To grandma enjoy this book!
Naomi xx

CW01656329

West Yorkshire

Edited by Lisa Adlam & Mark Richardson

First published in Great Britain in 2010 by
Young Writers
Remus House
Coltsfoot Drive
Peterborough
PE2 9JX
Telephone: 01733 890066
Website: www.youngwriters.co.uk

All Rights Reserved
Book Design by Spencer Hart
© Copyright Contributors 2009
SB ISBN 978-1-84924-771-9

Foreword

At Young Writers our defining aim is to promote an enjoyment of reading and writing amongst children and young adults. By giving aspiring poets the opportunity to see their work in print, their love of the written word as well as confidence in their own abilities has the chance to blossom.

Our latest competition Poetry Explorers was designed to introduce primary school children to the wonders of creative expression. They were given free reign to write on any theme and in any style, thus encouraging them to use and explore a variety of different poetic forms.

We are proud to present the resulting collection of regional anthologies which are an excellent showcase of young writing talent. With such a diverse range of entries received, the selection process was difficult yet very rewarding. From comical rhymes to poignant verses, there is plenty to entertain and inspire within these pages. We hope you agree that this collection bursting with imagination is one to treasure.

Contents

Ashlands Primary School

Bramley St Peter's CE Primary School

Churwell Primary School

Micklefield CE Primary School

St Augustine's RC Primary School, Leeds

Stanningley Primary School

Swinnow Primary School

The Poems

My Mad Monkey Cousin

We arrived today
At our place for a peaceful holiday,
Or what I thought would be.
We arrived today
At our place for a noisy holiday,
With my mad monkey cousin.
My cute little cousin is not what she seems,
All day she bounces and screams,
I know the truth,
I know what she is,
She's not a little toddler
With curly, blonde hair,
She's my mad monkey cousin.
One day while we lay in the sun
My mad monkey cousin
Came toddling along,
She had a puzzle in her hands,
'In The Night Garden' it said,
I shuddered at the thought that popped in my head,
I tiptoed away before she picked me to help her.
With her usual victims gone
She chose my brother,
But he was foolish enough to refuse.
I looked up from my fake distraction,
Her eyes were red,
Her teeth were bared,
From then on he was forced to help her
With every single need.
She never paid him with one break,
He was forever in her little shadow.

Maggie Pearson (10)
Ashlands Primary School

My Brother The Orang-Utan

My brother the orang-utan
Sits happily on his branch
His eyes zooming this way and that
As he searches his territory for his favourite toy
And then he stops
He can hear a creaking
Another animal approaching
His body tenses
Ready for anything
A black monkey enters the area
The orang-utan leaps into the air howling
'Get out of my room!'
The monkey jumps in surprise
The orang-utan swings his arms in a frenzy
The monkey darts away and the
Orang-utan relaxes, his glossy red fur shines in the sunlight
A big grin splits over his face
He sneaks down his branch and pads
Slowly through the jungle
When he reaches his destination
He carefully opens the treat cupboard
And takes every last thing!
He runs back to his branch
Grinning
When Mum finds out
I get the blame
And all this time
No one realises
It was my brother
The orang-utan.

Max McKinnon-Evans (10)
Ashlands Primary School

Falling Leaves

I love the sleeping trees at night and day.
When night awakes they brighten like day.

I watch the leaves swirling,
Crackling and twirling down
From the trees.

The tree's eyes peering out from
The earth to see the soggy ground.
The colour of the leaves changing, yellow
Golden and brown.

Cobwebs glistening in the sun and grass
Wet and shining and falling leaves.
Trees behind the sunset
Glimmering with leaves.

What a beautiful sight.
The leaves, they wait to fall to the ground.
Silver glimmering, the twigs dancing
And talking.

The wind whispering and swirling
Around and around you.
The wind swaying and
Blowing leaves around.

I love the wind and leaves
That shake until they fall down off the trees.
Every day they sway and sway.
I love all the different kinds of leaves.
Small, big, round, I don't mind at all.
Here comes autumn.

Kate White (8)
Ashlands Primary School

The Tiger

As you walk into her territory you hear a slight rustling,
As the tiger moves in her grassy lair.
As you lie down behind a grassy mound,
Waiting for your first lesson of hunting.
Then she begins, you follow and learn,
As you follow you learn she is a very energetic hunter.
You watch in horror as she viciously rips apart an antelope
And drags it back barely alive to her lair.

Later on the antelope is thrown out of the tiger's territory,
It slowly limps away, now it is your turn to hunt,
She comes and helps you on the way,
You can hunt properly now,
Sometimes she comes to see your catch and helps you eat it
Having not hunted herself. (A sign of old age perhaps?)

As you whisper to your friend,
She turns around and pounces, letting loose a terrible growl.
Eyes glinting with immense fury, you watch petrified.
Stuck to the ground and feebly crying out in pain,
As rows of razor sharp teeth clamp down on your arm.
Then she drags you out of her territory to be humiliated by passing
Animals.
Another cub is mean to you or attacks you,
She protects you and tears after her prey.
You hear a terrifying roar,
No one speaks, not a sound,
They all know the victim has been caught.

James Hodson (10)
Ashlands Primary School

A Mango - Haiku

A cold heart inside
Soft smooth Caribbean fruit
The bright morning sun.

Tia Fieldhouse (10)
Ashlands Primary School

Autumn

Summer bids farewell to the world
As Autumn takes her place
And the trees bare themselves
To the season's ruthless face.

Mother Nature walks this way
Dying the world golden brown
And sprinkling her with the icing-sugar frost
That adds the sparkle to her autumn gown.

Leaves crunch beneath humans' feet
As they walk through the dark woods
And squelching emanates from the path
For thick are the autumn muds.

Autumn flicks her flame-filled hair
And the bonfires shift in response
Her jewellery flashes in the garden embers
And the fireworks explode at once.

Wind whistles around corners
And wails down dark alleys
As children dressed as ghosts and ghouls
Trick or treat in English valleys.

Conkers compete to be the brightest
Squirrels collect food for the cold
Hedgehogs lie down for a long winter sleep
And Autumn . . . well, she grows old.

Skye Lury (11)
Ashlands Primary School

Apple - Haiku

Speckled grub for snack
Pull the stalk, set off grenade
Core, soft and juicy.

Daniel Pelkowski (10)
Ashlands Primary School

My Cousin - The Lion

My cousin - the lion
Is lying relaxed,
Lightly snoozing,
Preening her flowing locks.

A herd of zebra
Appear from around a corner
And snigger, 'Look! Her coat!
What an awful disgrace!'

'The planet should wear
Stripes just like us!'
They cry.
'Quiet Beth! I think she heard you.'

The lion slowly
Opens an eye,
Sees four tiny zebra
Hunched in a corner.

The other eye opens,
The zebras quiver.
'Oh gosh not us!
We're too young to die!'

'You're never
Too young
To be eaten by me.
The younger the juicier is what I always say!'

Josie Bedford (10)
Ashlands Primary School

Apple

Red with brown freckles on skin
Juice squirting when open
Rough spiky star underneath.

Victoria Sheehan (10)
Ashlands Primary School

My Teacher, The Tiger

My teacher, the tiger
Is waiting
Waiting
Waiting impatiently for her feast
A herd of deer enters
Some timid
Some playful
But all wary
They take their places
The tiger is watchful
She prowls silently around
Pondering who will be her victim today
'Homework please' the tiger growls
She licks her lips
She knows dinner is soon
'Matthew, where is your homework?'
The deer pleads pathetically for its life
Too late
The tiger pounces
A snarling frenzy ensues
The other deer flinch
Shuffling deeper into their seats
They're safe now
Until
Next time.

Class 6GC
Ashlands Primary School

Joy

The colour of joy is blue because it is the colour of a balloon.
Joy looks like a bear.
Joy feels like a cushion.
Joy sounds like a guitar.
Joy smells like a cake.

Elliot Thompson (7)
Ashlands Primary School

Goodbye Mr Autumn

As I walk into Mr Autumn's
Footsteps I can see all the trees
Snuggling into their winter coats,
Dancing and prancing with the
Auburn leaves as they fall doing
Pirouettes from the trees' hair.

The sap smiling sweetly
As it jumps out and runs
Down the chocolate road.
The crackling fire in autumn
Hair licking at the wood as
It spits but soon it will die.

However, ahead of him lies the
Tangy pumpkins laughing with their
Evil, jagged mouths and brains of fire.
The chocolate drops falling from the green, lush sky.

The bees fighting for clothes
As they stand there bare and nude,
But before their eyes, Jack Frost returns.
The wind whistling a tune - goodnight Mr Autumn,
Goodbye Mr Autumn.

Thomas Everett (10)
Ashlands Primary School

Sadness

Sadness is grey like a rusty dustbin lid.
Sadness tastes of grass from the field.
Sadness smells of rotting fish.
Sadness sounds like church bells tolling.
Sadness feels like hard rock.
Sadness reminds me of an old, abandoned house.
Sadness looks like a grey, stormy sky.

Samuel Speed (7)
Ashlands Primary School

Autumn Poem

He is here,
He makes me see
The sparkling fireworks,
The leaves he's thrown,
The bare trees he's stripped,
The people wrapped up warm.

He makes me smell
The damp leaves he ignored,
The crispy, scarlet leaves,
The smoky bonfire,
The sizzling sausages on the stove.

He makes me hear
The crackling of the bonfire,
The crunchy leaves beneath my feet,
The wind he's blown whispering in my ear,
The people screaming at the beauty of it all.

He makes me feel
The cool breeze on my cheek,
The fluffy gloves on my hand,
The warmth from the sparkler,
The hard leaves brushing against my legs.

Ellie Coones (10)
Ashlands Primary School

Silence

Silence tastes like green broccoli that I have for tea.
Silence sounds like thunder and lightning you see on a cloudy day.
Silence reminds me of a jungle with not a single animal in it.
Silence feels like a smooth stone that I pick up by the seaside.
Silence is the colour orange that you eat.
Silence smells like a burning fish in the oven.
Silence looks like a school with noisy children in it.

Eve Snowdon (8)
Ashlands Primary School

Kestrel

The kestrel is coming,
Swooping across the field,
She has spotted us mice
Scampering around near the hedgerow.

The kestrel is coming,
She hovers above us,
Then grabs at us
With her over-long, blood-coloured talons.

She flaps her wings,
We gasp for breath
And slowly, slowly,
We feel our feet leave the floor.

Up on the tree branch
We squirm and squiggle,
The kestrel asks us,
What we were doing.

We say nothing,
She gives us a warning
Then lets us go,
With scratches on our fur.

Katherine Francis (10)
Ashlands Primary School

My Joy Poem

I think joy is red because it is a hot feeling
Joy looks like a party or a wedding
Joy tastes like fresh, bright strawberries
Joy feels like a big, fluffy blanket because it makes me happy
Joy sounds like people laughing and having fun
Because joy is a happy time
Joy reminds me of people playing and having fun
Joy smells like a big piece of Pepperami pizza.

Esther Hilton (8)
Ashlands Primary School

The Wind In Autumn

Autumn is here and
The wind is coming out to play,
Rejoicing gaily that
His time has come.

He breathes a puff of
Fresh air and freezes
People to the bone.

He whistles a tune
While he teaches the
Orange dancers to twist
And whirl to the damp, spongy ground.

He waits and shouts
Down the chimney pot
Wanting to be let in
From the storm.

He grabs at the delightful
Smell of bacon butties
And pushes it over to tempt
A hungry, wet, miserable person
Who has been caught in the rain.

Joe Hesmondhalgh (10)
Ashlands Primary School

Love

Love is red, like a rose gleaming in the sun,
Love looks like someone kissing in the beautiful sunset,
Love tastes like candyfloss melting in your mouth,
Love smells of chocolate hearts and
beautiful red roses on someone's anniversary,
Love reminds me of my cat purring on my bed,
Love sounds like the high note of the bell from a church,
Love feels like a big heart-shaped cushion on my bed.

Katie MacGregor (8)
Ashlands Primary School

Autumn Poem

Squirrels run up the trees,
As leaves sadly fall.
I hear my shoes stepping on leaves,
'Ouch,' say the leaves.

Trees are sad as they're going bare,
Leaves are depressed.
I smell the cold air going up my nose,
It's breezy all around.

My monster mask for Hallowe'en
Frightens the little ones.
'I'm so scared,' shriek the leaves,
As I waltz down the street.

I taste my toffee apple
As I watch the dancing fire.
I hear it crackling all around
In the dark night.

The barks off the trees are rough,
I feel them with my cold hands.
The trees are shouting 'Come back leaves,'
As they shiver in the breeze.

John Cody (10)
Ashlands Primary School

Dog

Always on patrol of the school.
Helpful to everyone.
Do not anger her or she'll bark.
Always digging for information.
Dragging people into her dog house to be taught.
Growling at people that don't pay attention.
Keeping halls safe from people that don't respect it.
Strolling down the corridor while her prey is behind the tables.

Jake Allister (10)
Ashlands Primary School

My Sister The Monkey

My sister is a cheeky monkey,
She swings from her bed,
She stamps her feet,
Shouts out loud,
It really hurts your head.

My parents come in and say,
'Helen keep it down!
Stop stamping your feet,
You are a cheeky monkey,
Keep your feet on the ground.'

My sister is a cheeky monkey,
She trails a great big mess,
I say 'Helen tidy your room,
Clear up your clothes.'
She says 'I really need to rest.'
My sister is a cheeky monkey
But when she goes to sleep,
It feels like she could sleep forever,
Because she doesn't make a peep.

Gemma Levesley (11)
Ashlands Primary School

Happiness Poem

Happiness is the colour of green, fresh, dewy, soft grass.
Happiness looks like a rainbow high in the sky.
Happiness tastes like bacon, crispy on my tongue.
Happiness smells like fresh sausages
just come off the barbecue on a hot summer's day.
Happiness feels like a soft, cuddly rabbit against your palm.
Happiness reminds me of a clown and the audience
bursting with laughter.
Happiness sounds like beautiful music
played by the harp, ringing out.

Sam McKinnon-Evans (8)
Ashlands Primary School

The Magic Of The Brain

Such a sight I saw:
Crashing waves smashing against the side of the boat.
Small, still waves just passing by.
Such a sight I saw.

Such a sound I heard:
Fishes jumping out of the water.
The boat is going side to side.
Such a sound I heard.

Such a smell I smelled:
The salty, sparkling water swishing around.
The smell of fresh fish makes me hungry.
Smell of suncream on people.
Such a smell I smelled.

Such a feeling I felt:
I felt the soft sand in my hand.
I felt the spiky shell on my hand.
A jagged rock I stood on.
Such a feeling felt.

Kate Nixon (10)
Ashlands Primary School

Autumn's Coming

Autumn's coming, it's on its way,
Trees are waiting for their leaves
To fly down and then they turn a
Shiny red or brown, some of them
Might look a bit rusty even though
They're not.
Then they start to get kicked by people,
Everything gets chaotic.

This is what I love about autumn,
Because it's just amazing.

James Hawkshaw (8)
Ashlands Primary School

The Red Squirrel

The red squirrel comes,
Scurrying along.
The tree branch making her
Claws go *tap, tap, tap.*

She is always hoarding nuts
For her kittens' rewards.
But one paw out of line
And she bites down.

Her far-fetched
Funny chatter
Goes on for days
And days.

Red squirrels are rare,
You'll never see anyone like her,
Always protecting you,
But can bite!

Niamh Egars (10)
Ashlands Primary School

Autumn

It is autumn and the tired sun has drawn its curtains
While the shedding trees have put their autumn
Clothes on.

It is autumn and the flames of the bonfire are
Trying to lash out at the people who are being
Tempted by the toffee apples.

It is autumn and the night is lit by the glowing
Orange skull decorations that have been cut off
Their bodies, while the trick or treaters' costumes
Come to life.

It is autumn.

Stephane Trouille (10)
Ashlands Primary School

My Baby Cousin Is A Gibbon

She sits and stares as a cute as can be
Charming us all
Sucking us all into a world of daze
Then suddenly
We don't realise
But she's off
Yap, yap, yap
We're all broken from the daze
Unstoppable
Surprised
Shocked
The silence
She's off again
On a round of attention-seeking
Sucking on her scream stopper
We think she's cute (she is)
But my baby cousin is a gibbon!

Ned Hilton (10)
Ashlands Primary School

The Octopus

The octopus sits waiting for a new victim,
Watching over the whole school.
Slowly tentacles slither out of the sea cave,
Gathering speed, she slides down the corridor.
Approaching her victim's classroom she pulls open the door.
She speaks solemnly as an evil smile spreads across her face.
'Is James Dillon in this classroom?'
Slowly a small child gets up
And his face white with fear as he mumbles, 'H-here.'
She lashes out quickly and says, 'Won't be long,' in her cold voice.
She drags the victim off to her sea cave and after that
All that is heard is a small choking sound.
No one dares speak of that deadly hour.

William Rowe (10)
Ashlands Primary School

Autumn Is A Magical Time

I watch the leaves from my room,
Under the big, round harvest moon.
Watching the leaves clinging onto the branches.
They go red to brown, brown to rusty, rusty to golden,
But they can't cling on forever.
So at last the howling and screaming wind blows them off the trees.
But as they fall they all look like they are waving.
Farewell to summer.
So when they carefully touch the ground,
They create a magical carpet on the ground,
And when Mother Nature steps on the ground, the leaves
Make a magical sound, the sound that the crackling fire makes.
She spreads frost onto the ground, it makes the ground glisten,
And after her hard day's work she and her kitten snuggle up by
The fire.
They drink hot cocoa and eat crisp, brown nuts.
Finally she falls asleep.

Olivia Kahlon (8)
Ashlands Primary School

Where Has Summer Gone?

Looking out my bedroom window I can see the seasons changing.
The whistling wind blowing round the house,
The faint little noises of the hibernating mouse.
The chimney smoke curling round,
The conkers that my sister found.
The gold, brown, rusty leaves scattered on the floor,
The freezing cold hailstones tapping at the door.
The spiky bare trees swaying in the rain,
The next door neighbours' smoky bonfire flame.
The frozen pond all icy blue,
The sparkly spiderweb all covered in dew.
There were signs of summer but now there are none,
Where, oh where has the summer gone?

Elizabeth Francis (9)
Ashlands Primary School

The Moonlight Web

As the pitter-patter of the rain pings down on my window
I put on my slippers and dressing gown
And tiptoe down to my window
I creak open the shutters
And look all around
I see the pearl-white moon
And the moonlit damp grass
But there underneath my window ledge
I see a moonlight web
Its knitting so delicate and made with care
The water looks like snowdrops
In the dusky moon
And with a glance I see it all
So silver and majestic
I wish for it to be here forever
So I named it my moonlight web
Knowing I'll see it soon . . .

Olivia Jones (10)
Ashlands Primary School

The Spider

One night I go to my room.
I see a web dangling from the roof,
Then a spider comes and stares.
I dare not move as it comes closer,
Then I shout 'Mum!' in a little voice.
The spider comes closer
So I shout 'Mum!' a little louder.
The spider stops and hangs on its web,
Then I walk backwards to the door.
Then I shout 'Mum!' She comes in
And does the most dreadful scream ever
And runs out of my bedroom, I do the same.
I am never going in my bedroom again!

Ben Moorhouse (10)
Ashlands Primary School

After Summer

It's the end of summer,
The leaves are dancing,
The trees are waving,
The wind is wailing,
The squirrels are scattering.
The conkers are cracking
And the leaves are laughing.
Trees whistle towards the ground.
The sun is fading
And the clouds are coming.
Longer nights, shorter days.
Leaves change colour.
Hibernation starts.
Trees sway like they are trying to tell secrets.
Sycamore keys hanging onto their trees and then
Twirl down, trying to fly back,
To make the most of autumn.

Nathan Foster (9)
Ashlands Primary School

It's Autumn

A fire-lord is awakening
Autumn sounds the horn of hibernation
As insects migrate to where summer is a-plenty
Autumn pulls leaves off trees
Showering the earth in burning paper.

Autumn speaks with the voice of a thousand fireworks
Bringing joy and fear across the land
Autumn slips on his cloak of fire, red and orange
And his cloak of shadow.

September is a holiday for insects
October offers fear and superstition
November brings back Guy Fawkes.

Nathan Fong (10)
Ashlands Primary School

Autumn Poem

Autumn is here,
His inky black nights surrounding us.
The autumn leaves lie flat on the
Luscious grass.
The leaves are dancing in the midnight air.

Autumn is here,
He whistled the flowing wind,
He blew the dull clouds,
He changed from his
Summer clothes to autumn.

Autumn is here,
He can taste the sweet
Fire steaming in his mouth.
Soon the trees will turn into
Their winter clothes and new
Changes will begin.

Hannah Haw (10)
Ashlands Primary School

Silence

Silence is the colour grey.
Silence looks like a class of children
Reading in their heads.
Silence tastes like a drip of water
Dropping into my mouth.
Silence smells like a gust of wind
Blowing up my nostrils.
Silence sounds like a gust of wind
Howling in my ear.
Silence feels like a blanket rubbing
Against my hand.
Silence reminds me of a cold winter's day.

Daniel Hawthorn (8)
Ashlands Primary School

Autumn

It's autumn again and the towns and cities are hidden by leaves,
They are playing here, there and everywhere,
And just when you clean them up,
The wind comes along and snatches the pile
and hurls them everywhere.

It's autumn and Hallowe'en owes us a visit
And it is hard to resist the toffee apples,
All they say is, 'Eat me, eat me.'
Wherever you look you see pumpkins giving you an evil glare
And their eyes seem to follow your every move.
Ding dong! Ding dong!
Is all you hear as the doorbells tell us someone is here.

Now autumn is going. It waves us goodbye till next year
But winter shoves him off his feet and yells with a devilish look
'I'm back.'

Joe Tales (10)
Ashlands Primary School

My Friend The Kitten

He walks round waiting for his playmate
Then he will pounce and claw at a toy,
Then he will come and be nice and
Want you to stroke him.
But really
When you are not there
He will approach the kitchen table
And eat what he can find.
When you look for the missing food,
The cat will look innocently and purr
And who should be blamed but the poor
Puppy dog!

Kieran Kurtalan (10)
Ashlands Primary School

My Joy Poem

Joy looks like a diamond ring being blared at by the sun as it reflects back at you and attempts to blind you.

Joy tastes like marshmallows that have just been toasted on a hot summer's day while the cool breeze makes it colder.

Joy reminds me of my first ever teddy bear, just holding it made me feel warm inside, it reminded me of the first time I cuddled it.

Joy smells like purple lavender, fresh, just picked from the garden.

The colour of joy is a pale green, the green of a stem of a sunflower that has just blossomed.

Joy sounds like someone ripping open the wrapping paper on Christmas Day and getting exactly what they asked for and everybody is full of joy as the snow falls on their heads.

Joy feels like an Aston Martin, it is as smooth as smooth can be.

Ralph Atkinson (9)
Ashlands Primary School

The Cheetah

The cheetah runs wild round and round,
Always there watching you no matter what,
When she walks strolling up and down,
Always got people to play with,
Striding at 50 miles an hour,
At a tremendous speed,
Being healthy, actively playing games.
Never just watching you normally using her beady eyes,
Never just sitting there,
Arguing sometimes, playing other times
Knowing everything, never not knowing things,
Always got something to say.

Becky Spink (10)
Ashlands Primary School

In The Night

Me abroad
All tucked up in bed
No fears
No dread
Nothing to see
Nothing to hear
Or wait, is there?

My one, only fear
The one little pest
A little mosquito
At its best
I turn it on, the one dreaded buzzing sound
But only to know my sister's awake
'Turn it off now
I've had enough of your mess-arounds.'

Elizabeth Rudge (10)
Ashlands Primary School

Five Senses

I like the taste of chocolate
Melting in my mouth.

I like the smell of pancakes
Sizzling in the pan.

I like the sound of music
Playing *full blast.*

I like the feeling of grass
Tickling my feet.

I like the look of trees
Towering over me.

Emma Jones (9)
Ashlands Primary School

Five Senses

I like taste of lobster,
Chewing every bit.

I like the smell of pancakes
Shooting up my nose.

I like the feel of the sea
Rising upon my feet.

I like the sound of birds
Tweeting in the morning.

I like the look of snowflakes
Falling outside my window.

Toby Woodman (9)
Ashlands Primary School

Five Senses

I like the taste of fizzy sweets
Fizzing on my tongue.

I like the smell of pizza
Rushing into my nose.

I like the feeling of mud
Splashing onto my face.

I like the sound of trains
Clattering over the rails.

I like the look of blue sky
Peeking through the clouds.

Harry Hunt (9)
Ashlands Primary School

Five Senses

I like the taste of crisps
Crunching in my mouth.

I like the smell of a Chinese
Emptying my stomach.

I like the feel of silk
Tickling my hand.

I like the sound of laughter
Meaning everyone is happy.

I like the look of fireworks
Exploding in the sky.

Edward Martin (9)
Ashlands Primary School

Five Senses

I like the smell of Bolognaise
Wriggling in my mouth.

I like the smell of paper
Flowing up my nose.

I like the feel of chilli
Burning in my mouth.

I like the sound of a Lotus
Roaring on the road.

I like the look of monkeys
Swinging in the trees.

Nicholas Ducker (9)
Ashlands Primary School

Five Senses

I like the taste of chocolate
Melting on my tongue.

I like the smell of pizza
Burning in the oven.

I like the feel of snow
Crunching under my feet.

I like the sound of the piano
Playing in my ears.

I like the look of my friends
Smiling away.

Francesca Woodman (9)
Ashlands Primary School

Five Senses

I like the taste of ice lollies
Melting in my mouth.

I like the smell of chocolate chips
Baking in the oven.

I like the feel of grass
Brushing against my leg.

I like the sound of the wind
Howling past my ears.

I like the look of fish
Jumping out of the water.

Samantha Phillips (9)
Ashlands Primary School

Five Senses

I like the taste of ice cream
Melting in my mouth.

I like the smell of casserole
Cooking on the heater.

I like the feel of bubbles
Popping on my hand.

I like the sound of birds
Singing in the morning.

I like the look of the moon
Glowing in my bedroom.

Ellie Mason (9)
Ashlands Primary School

Five Senses

I like the taste of chocolate
Melting in my mouth.

I like the smell of vanilla
Spreading from place to place.

I like the sound of the sea
Rippling on the shore.

I like the feel of sand
Rubbing on my feet.

I like the look of fireworks
Exploding in the sky.

Matilda Webster (9)
Ashlands Primary School

Autumn Senses

As the hedgehog walks down the road. . .
He sees the trees changing their clothes to maple red.

As the hedgehog sleeps he hears. . .
The autumn spirit changing the leaves.

As the hedgehog scurries around he smells. . .
The burning fire, leaping in the air.

As the hedgehog feasts on berries. . .
He tastes the Hallowe'en treats ahead.

As the hedgehog gets ready for winter. . .
He feels the hardworking earthworms mining tunnels.

Edward Merrett (10)
Ashlands Primary School

Five Senses

I like the taste of ice cubes
Melting on my tongue.

I like the smell of dough balls
Blowing up my nose.

I like the feel of rain
Tapping on my face.

I like the sound of thunder
Banging in my ears.

I like the look of eyes
Glowing in the dark.

Rachel Flint (9)
Ashlands Primary School

Five Senses

I like the taste of crumble,
Crumbling in my mouth.

I like the smell of perfume,
Whizzing up my nose.

I like the feel of my duvet,
Wrapping me up tight.

I like the sound of gravel,
Crunching under a car wheel.

I like the look of a mountain's peak
Towering above me.

Jemima Spence (9)
Ashlands Primary School

Five Senses

I like the taste of chocolate
Melting in my mouth.

I like the smell of wood
Burning through my nose.

I like the feel of snow
Drizzling on my tongue.

I like the sound of rain
Crashing down from the sky.

I like the look of the sun
Shining through the clouds.

Charlotte Simpson (9)
Ashlands Primary School

Five Senses

I like the taste of milkshake
Rushing down my throat.

I like the smell of sausages
Sizzling in the pan.

I like the feel of my cat
Lying on my lap.

I like the sound of birds
Twittering past.

I like the look of popcorn
Popping In the microwave.

Otis Newell (9)
Ashlands Primary School

Five Senses

I like the taste of apples
Crunching in my mouth.

I like the smell of spring
Blowing at my nose.

I like the feel of sand
Running on my toes.

I like the sound of the sea
Rumbling in my ears.

I like the look of the moon
Sparkling at night.

Isla Lury (9)
Ashlands Primary School

Five Senses

I like the taste of bacon
Sizzling on my tongue.

I like the smell of bonfires
Licking at my nose.

I like the feel of rain
Pouring on my face.

I like the sound of music
Rushing round my ears.

I like the look of people
Writing in their books.

Thomas Harris (9)
Ashlands Primary School

Five Senses

I like the taste of chocolate drizzling
Down my throat.

I like the smell of pizza when I draw it
To my mouth.

I like the feel of cat fur
Brushing against my legs.

I like the sound of chicks
Chirping in my ear.

I like the look of the countryside
Beaming in my eyes.

Adam Wilcox (9)
Ashlands Primary School

Five Senses

I like the taste of Galaxy chocolate
Melting in my mouth.

I like the smell of fire
Burning down a match.

I like the feel of prawn crackers
Popping in my mouth.

I like the sound of music
Playing in my ears.

I like the look of the sea
Splashing everyone on the beach.

Alex Barrett (9)
Ashlands Primary School

Five Senses

I like the taste of pizza
Sizzling in my mouth.

I like the smell of chlorine
Rushing through my nose.

I like the feel of soft blankets
Sliding across my skin.

I like the sound of music
Dancing in my ears.

I like the look of colourful art
Lighting up my eyes.

Alastair Clarke (9)
Ashlands Primary School

My Dad The Shark

My dad the shark
My dad the shark is fishing for breakfast
He is getting ready to pounce
He pounces!
His fins skim the water
The fish swim for their lives
None of them survive
On a full stomach he sets off for work
He cuts open cars with his top fin
Then he crushes the car back together
And walks away, ready for his lunch.

Richard Hale (10)
Ashlands Primary School

Silence

Silence is black and blue like my teddy bear.
Silence looks like a person in a cave who has just found a ruby.
Silence tastes like you have just eaten
a bowl of chips and fish fingers.
Silence smells like sticky toffee pudding
that has just come out of the oven.
Silence sounds like a class of children
that are telling a story at the end of the school day.
Silence feels like someone ringing the bell on a rainy school day.
Silence reminds me of my mum and dad reading me a story
when I am snuggled up with my hot water bottle.

Daniel Rowe (8)
Ashlands Primary School

The Bear Teacher

The bear sits in her den in peace, working busily.
Suddenly a whisper breaks the silence,
She lets out a growl of warning.
The sound continues.
The prey looks up at the empty den and his eyes grow wide.
Anxiously, he scans the room for any sign of the predator.
A large shadow looms over the prey.
She seizes her prey and drags it out of the room.
Her cubs stare in horror.
There's a roar of anger.
And then silence.

Ethan Thompson (10)
Ashlands Primary School

It's Autumn

It's autumn
And the trees are changing their clothes,
They are all saying 'Hello my autumn friends.'

All the family of acorns are coming off the trees and all of the animals are collecting food,
They are going to the supermarket.

Autumn wears brown boots with brown and orange crinkly trousers.
They are beginning to wear their winter clothes.

All of the conkers are banging their heads.

Jessica Ackroyd (10)
Ashlands Primary School

An Autumn Poem

Autumn is here, he has changed his summer clothing
And the tree leaves autumn shades.

And at the end of the day, Autumn is exhausted and inks the
Sky and dots stars across the night sky.

As the leaves fall into the autumn ponds, Autumn comes
Trick or treating to our doors.

Soon the trees will be bare, pumpkins outside feeling abandoned.
Soon Autumn's work will be done. But little does he know it's
Going to happen again next year.

Ghislaine Cross (10)
Ashlands Primary School

Our Vulture Teacher - Haikus

Circling her pupils,
Diving at any mistake,
Eyeing everyone.

Anyone naughty,
She uses her evil stare,
Fixing on her prey.

Suddenly she sees,
She swoops at misbehaviour,
Punishment: 'Miss break!'

Kate Bacon (10)
Ashlands Primary School

My Brother The Snake

He slithers around looking for his prey
When he finds his victim
He coils himself and waits
For it to enter his territory.

The snake licks his lips
The deadly look of it
He hypnotises his prey
His teeth slowly appear
Until he pounces on his prey . . .

Max Tales (10)
Ashlands Primary School

Autumn

It's autumn
And the trees are changing the colour of their clothes.
The conkers have been dropped from the arms of the tree
And the leaves are speaking with their slow
And steady voice to the trees.

The tree is wearing a range of different colours
And they are falling from the tree.
Winter is coming now, the leaves are hiding
From his petrifying yet sluggish performance.

Sanita Ranu (11)
Ashlands Primary School

Sadness Poem

Sadness looks like a girl alone crying.
Sadness is the colour of a marshmallow.
Sadness reminds me of an ice cream.
Sadness tastes of a stick of candyfloss.
Sadness smells of fish and chips.

Phoebe Spence (7)
Ashlands Primary School

Leopard

The leopard strolls to her cubs and drags her prey to the den.
There no cub knows what goes on.
She plays with the cubs but makes sure they're not carried away.
She chases other creatures off and growls when she disapproves.
The leopard teaches them to run, catch, hunt.
Her children chase butterflies and bees. . .
While she watches them with fondness.
As the day dawns she sends them back to their real parents.
She knows that one day she won't see them at her class.

Sophie Bolton (10)
Ashlands Primary School

My Teacher The Spider

My teacher the spider is waiting,
Waiting for her prey to come into her lair.
One by one she gobbles them up
Until there are no insects left.
Then she gets angry.
She waits and waits,
Then one insect comes,
She grabs him and spins him up.
She slowly eats him limb by limb.

Matthew Connolly (10)
Ashlands Primary School

Fun

Fun reminds me of my daddy's teddy called White Ted.
Fun is the colour yellow because it's happy and it makes me giggle.
Fun sounds like raining money, falling from the sky.
Fun tastes like marshmallows melting in my mouth.
Fun looks like teddies alive hugging each other.
Fun feels like bouncing on my trampoline.

Samuel Bretherick (7)
Ashlands Primary School

Joy

Joy is the colour of orange like the oranges.
Joy looks like everyone having a snow fight.
Joy reminds me of running in a field and then coming in drinking hot cocoa in a cup.
Joy sounds like summer shouting in the air.
Joy smells of a steam train on holiday hooting and steam spitting out.
Joy feels like touching a fork, eating tea in the winter snuggled up.
Joy tastes like toast on a spring morning.

Adam Hayes (9)
Ashlands Primary School

Autumn Attacks

Autumn attacks the trees and so they lose their leaves.
The skeletons of the trees wait for their new coats.
The brown crisp leaves rot on the empty trees.

Cartwheel fireworks like chariot wheels,
And others like knights throwing flaming gold spears.
They shoot through the sky like cannonballs.

But then! It's time for autumn to
Pack away its toys and go away!

Tom Boggins (10)
Ashlands Primary School

Kiwi - Haikus

A canoe in a
Green lagoon, with ebony
Paddles by the side.

A cream clam opened,
Protecting a small round pearl,
Laid in green water.

Alix Clarkson (10)
Ashlands Primary School

The Gorilla

Stumbling down the corridor, the gorilla
Retreats to his frost classroom.

Occasionally other small monkeys hear his deep,
Ferocious voice echoing along the wild corridor.
The beast is petrifying.

Humorously the gorilla munches on bananas and apples,
Leaving a trail of banana skins on the grass
And apple juice and crushed plants all over.

Wesley Ryan (10)
Ashlands Primary School

The Tree

I changed my clothes
From a bright vibrant green
To a lifeless, gloomy brown.
My friends and family would say
Goodbye just before they departed.

Occasionally I would look up and
I would see wonderful creatures.
They dance to the noises of the night.

Sam Crocombe (10)
Ashlands Primary School

Silence Poem

Silence is the colour of white and yellow
Silence tastes like a toffee melting in my mouth
Silence smells of my bed covers when they have just been washed
Silence sounds like my bedroom in the middle of the night
Silence feels like a soft, warm blanket on top of me
Silence reminds me of my baby niece
Sleeping in her Moses basket.

Charley Addy (8)
Ashlands Primary School

Autumn Poem

It's autumn, the bonfire is lit
He paints the leaves from gold to
Black and licks the wood as it burns.

The bonfire weaves his colourful
Flames through the black fabric
Around him till he can't
Fight the darkness anymore. . .
And slowly he fades away.

Callum Kurtalan (10)
Ashlands Primary School

Autumn

Leaves falling down from the sky, red, gold and brown
The wind blows the leaves up and twirls them all around
The wind makes the leaves scared by the loud, howling sound
People step on the dry, dead leaves that make a crunching
Crackling sound
Children collecting conkers opening the spiky shells
Cold, crisp air with a chilly breeze
Autumn is here.

Rosa Cooper (8)
Ashlands Primary School

Love Poem

Love smells of splendid strawberries hanging on a tree.
Love is the colour of a sunset changing to a night sky.
Love tastes like a sweet orange tingling in my mouth.
Love sounds like people giggling with happiness.
Love feels like a gold glass heart.
Love reminds me of my family being joyful.
Love looks like a big gold mine with silver, bronze and gold.

Helen Levesley (7)
Ashlands Primary School

Love

Love feels like cherry tomatoes.
Love reminds me of Mum kissing Mark.
Love looks like a heart flying.
Love tastes like a muffin.
Love sounds like a heart beating.
Love smells like fish and chips.
The colour of love is red.

Ryan Thatcher (7)
Ashlands Primary School

Love Poem

Love looks like the sunset hovering over the horizon.
Love is pink like a blossoming rose.
Love makes me think of hearts flying in the sun.
Love tastes of marshmallows melting in your mouth.
Love smells like dry, washed clothes silky and warm.
Love sounds like birds singing in the treetops.
Love feels like cuddling up under your cover at night.

Poppy White (8)
Ashlands Primary School

Fun

Fun is yellow like the hot sizzling sun.
Fun looks like snow twinkling in the sky.
Fun tastes of candyfloss dissolving in your mouth.
Fun smells of potato wedges cooking in the oven.
Fun sounds like music playing in my ear.
Fun reminds me of children playing and dancing at a party.
Fun feels like a soft marshmallow, creamy and delicious.

Louise Cody (7)
Ashlands Primary School

The Mysterious Kiwi - Haikus

Ebony fishes
On a beautiful round lake
With dark green water.

A secret pearl in
Dark green water it lies with
Black fish all around.

Kate Bailey (10)
Ashlands Primary School

Silence

Silence is the colours blue and black.
Silence looks like people sleeping.
Silence tastes like a warm hot chocolate in front of the TV.
Silence smells like a small river rolling alongside the bank.
Silence reminds me of a wet day on Saturday and Sunday.
Silence feels like everyone is quiet.

Lorna Manville (7)
Ashlands Primary School

It's Autumn

It's autumn
And the trees are changing the colour of their clothes
And the trees are throwing conkers off their branches
And landing on the ground in their green pointy armour.
Hallowe'en's here, trick or treat sweets everywhere.
On a dark, gloomy night ghosts and Frankensteins everywhere.

Ethan Russell (10)
Ashlands Primary School

Happiness

Happiness is pale pink.
Happiness looks like people laughing.
Happiness tastes like soft marshmallows.
Happiness feels like kindness coming to you.
Happiness sounds like children playing at a party.
Happiness makes me remember a ladybird.

Kaitlin Harris (7)
Ashlands Primary School

It's Autumn

It's autumn and the leaves are jumping off the trees
And the fireworks jump up into the night sky.
As night falls and the snow jumps down,
And as the children lick their toffee apples,
The fireworks go up and explode
Into bright fireworks of colour.

Jake Sugden
Ashlands Primary School

Sadness

Sadness feels like a very bumpy ground.
Sadness looks like an armchair creaking in the night.
The colour of sadness is a very dark black paint drying in the sun.
Sadness tastes of your gums bleeding.
Sadness reminds me of fish dying in the sea.
Sadness smells of sausages burning in the oven.

Polly Bedford (7)
Ashlands Primary School

Joy

The colour of joy is purple
Joy feels like a balloon
Joy smells of fish and chips
Joy looks like people having a great time
Joy sounds like shouting
Joy reminds me of my kitten.

Charlie Robinson (8)
Ashlands Primary School

The Spider Who Ate The Dog

The spider who ate the dog
She thought he'd sleep on a log
When he grew fat
She looked like a bat
The spider who ate the dog

The spider was flat
But then she grew fat
Because she ate that fat dog
Indeed that dog tasted like a log

The spider who ate the dog
She thought he'd sleep on a log
When he grew fat
He looked like a bat
The spider who ate the dog

When the spider went into people's houses
They thought there was a mouse in the house
But he was a fat-looking mouse spider

The spider who ate the dog
She thought he'd sleep on a log
When he grew fat
She looked like a bat
The spider who ate the dog.

Rebecca Davies (9)
Bramley St Peter's CE Primary School

Fear Is Black, Like This Tale

There were five boys
playing tig in the dark
One ran into a house
but it was haunted

Bats, bats
Screaming
Screeching
Wolves howling
and ghosts surrounding

The door creaked shut
'Help, help!' the boy said

Bats, bats
Screaming
Screeching
Wolves howling
Ghosts surrounding

Floorboards creak
Lights flicker
Spiders and their webs all over

Bats, bats
Screaming
Screeching
Wolves howling
Ghosts surrounding.

Jayden Toole (9)
Bramley St Peter's CE Primary School

The Storm That Struck Our Boat

The storm struck the boat from side to side,
The lightning struck the flag with a big flash,
The waves wailed with fear.

The waves were undeniably nuts,
The lightning struck with fear,
The storm what struck,
The storm what struck,
The storm what struck our boat.

The rain poured and melted down,
The waves feared with a nasty groan,
The storm wailed with a mean frown.

The waves were undeniably nuts,
The lightning struck with fear,
The storm what struck,
The storm what struck,
The storm what struck our boat.

Hail storm fell down fast,
The boat creaked with a loud bang,
The storm wailed altogether.

The waves were undeniably nuts,
The lightning struck with fear,
The storm what struck,
The storm what struck,
The storm what struck our boat.

Melissa Sutcliffe
Bramley St Peter's CE Primary School

The Magic Horse

As I was walking on the beach one day,
I heard a horse saying neigh!
It glimpsed at me with sparkling eyes,
I hopped on her back, to my surprise
She took flight.

Over rooftops
Flew,
We flew.

The people below seemed so small,
Houses were the size of a tennis ball,
The sheep in the field were tiny dots,
About the size of Dalmatian spots,
It felt like the day wouldn't end.

Over rooftops
Flew,
We flew.

Then we landed by a farm,
The pony was still calm,
That was the best house for my friend,
She could live there until the end,
Best of all it's just round the bend.

Over rooftops
Flew,
We flew.

Anna Waterhouse (9)
Bramley St Peter's CE Primary School

My Caving Experience

Caving is really raving,
It really, really rocks,
Always mucky and dirty,
With water in your socks!

Stalactites hanging from the ceiling,
Gives me a really strange feeling,
Lion's canines pointing in your face,
Makes you feel like you need to run a race.

Stalagmites bulging up from the floor,
Really makes you want to see more,
The floor is infested with water,
Oh no . . . it's so deep it will make me shorter!

Gruesome, ghostly gaps,
That make you want to jump,
I'll have to go through, there's no other way . . .
So maybe you won't see me for another day.

I finally glimpsed daylight,
My heart raced like a stopwatch.
I was out, I was free,
My caving experience was a joy for me.

Caving is really raving,
It really, really rocks,
Always mucky and dirty,
With water in your socks.

Megan Kelsey Flaherty (11)
Bramley St Peter's CE Primary School

The Witching Hour

The cold, cold night,
The bright, bright light,
It's so quiet,
It must be 'the witching hour'.

It's dark, it's cold, it's night,
So don't come down to the Earth tonight,
So don't come down to the Earth tonight.

I'm scared,
I'm bare,
Also I'm hungry,
But it's still 'the witching hour'.

It's dark, it's cold, it's night,
So don't come down to the Earth tonight,
So don't come down to the Earth tonight.

There's no cars,
Or bars,
Not even a little white cat,
Hopefully though there's no rats,
Stuck in the grey dark drain,
But it's still 'the witching hour'.

It's dark, it's cold, it's night,
So don't come down to the Earth tonight,
So don't come down to the Earth tonight.

Caitlin Olivia Chivers (10)
Bramley St Peter's CE Primary School

About A Duck

In a pond I saw a duck
sticking her head in the water
but her neck was stuck
and a swan will have to support her.

Thomas Beaumont (9)
Bramley St Peter's CE Primary School

The Pony That Could Fly

There was a pony that could fly,
Indeed it flew so high in the sky.
Everyone was so amazed
By its wings that were being waved.
The pony was light blue just like the sky,
It also had a rainbow belt with sparkles.

The pony could fly,
So high in the sky,
She just whizzes by,
She's very, very cool,
Everyone likes her.

So the pony could fly,
People paid money to watch her cry.
Everyone wanted to stroke her fluffy, soft fur,
She was amazing,
She had a crown on her head with gleaming diamonds.

The pony could fly,
So high in the sky,
She just whizzes by,
She's very, very cool,
Everyone likes her.

Priya Kumari (9)
Bramley St Peter's CE Primary School

Monster At Our School

He walks around all day long,
The monster.
He sings his creepy song,
The monster.

He sits in the boiler room,
And you'll hear a *boom!*
Don't walk into the room,
Or he will say, 'You're in doom!'

He walks around all day long,
The monster.
He sings his creepy song,
The monster.

Don't get in his way,
Or you'll have to pay.
He thinks he's really cool,
But really he's a fool.

He walks around all day long,
The monster.
He sings his creepy song,
The monster.

Eden Mae Gillespie (11)
Bramley St Peter's CE Primary School

Extreme Orienteering

Orienteering to find the missing number,
Number code to find on the map,
Instructions! Easy!
Got to beat the other team,
Ingleborough like a jungle,
Race for the pole!
Boots killing me, dodging pot holes,
Blistered and soggy feet . . .

Prince Moyo (10)
Bramley St Peter's CE Primary School

My Little Pony

My little pony
has an uncle Tony
She's always fantastic
everybody likes her

My little pony
has a little coaty
She looks fabulous
everybody loves her

My little pony
has an uncle Tony
She's always fantastic
everybody likes her

As it comes to an end
my little pony ends
I'm so upset
I'm so, so wet

My little pony
had an uncle Tony
She was always fantastic
everybody cried.

Tiffany Earnshaw (9)
Bramley St Peter's CE Primary School

The Monster In Our School

There's a freaky creature in our school
There's trails from his drool
He hides in corners and acts cool
I know he lives in the storage room

People go down there every night
I'm surprised he doesn't give them a bite
And all the time I go down
I always wear a frightened frown

He's got a huge beady eye
With wings that help him fly
He screams and shouts
When he moves about

People go down there every night
I'm surprised he doesn't give them a bite
And all the time I go down
I always wear a frightened frown

One day I heard a scream
A bang, a thud, I knew he'd been seen
I looked round with a glare
And I noticed he wasn't there.

Caitlin Rennard (10)
Bramley St Peter's CE Primary School

The Monster In Our School

There's a monster in our school
who lives in the boiler room
He plays it very cool
but I'm no fool.

I go down every night
hoping for a really good fight
but if he's not there
the next day I'll give him an almighty stare.

He's green and smelly
and I named him Kelly
but he's really a boy
you really shouldn't annoy
So don't do that or he'll get you with a bat.

I go down there every night
hoping for a really good fight
but if he is not there
the next day I'll give you an almighty stare.

The teachers found out about the monster
so a boy gave them a tip
seal the boiler room with a clip.

Thomas Dawson
Bramley St Peter's CE Primary School

Silence

Silence is as dark as a cave
As dark as my friend's hair, Dave
Silence is as peaceful as day
Silence is not like hay

Silence, silence, silence
No one likes silence
Silence, silence, silence
It has no licence

'Silence!' says my teacher
I thought she was a creature
I wish she'd move house
'Cause I feel like a mouse

Silence, silence, silence
No one likes silence
Silence, silence, silence
It has no licence

Silence is a foe to us
In other words, me and Dave
So, silence go away and catch the bus
Silence is as dark as a cave.

Jordan Palfreyman (9)
Bramley St Peter's CE Primary School

My Model

My model is paint,
My model is material,
My model is sparkly.

The paint is slimy like a dog's drooling mouth,
Also, the paint is like microwaved, melted rainbows.

My model is paint,
My model is material,
My model is sparkly.

The material is silky soft like a spider's web,
The wallpaper's mine,
The wool is white as snow from above.

My model is paint,
My model is material,
My model is sparkly.

The glitter is like sparkly stars at night,
The glitter is so sticky, it's as if it's a toffee apple.

My model is paint,
My model is material,
My model is sparkly.

Megan Alice Lambert (11)
Bramley St Peter's CE Primary School

A Pony Who Ate An Elephant

A pony had a problem
A pony couldn't eat
She went to the doctor's
They asked her what was the problem
She said, 'Because I ate an elephant.'

A pony, a pony
Had a problem
A pony, a pony
Ate an elephant.

He said, 'Why are you so fat?
People say you look like a baseball bat'
She said, 'I feel sick!'
But in a tick
She was sick
So that is the end of the elephant pony.

A pony, a pony
Had a problem
A pony, a pony
Ate an elephant.

Millie Beaumont (9)
Bramley St Peter's CE Primary School

The Caves

The caves are cold,
The caves are spooky,
But the caves are mysterious.

The water is everywhere just like my shadow,
The water is dripping like rain,
The water is a hundred angels fluttering in my face.

The stalactites are sharp, slimy and jagged,
They are icicles hanging from above,
The stalactites are mine.

The caves are cold,
The caves are spooky,
But the caves are mysterious.

The rocks are as slippery as ice,
They are mine,
But there wasn't a fox around the rocks.

The caves are cold,
The caves are spooky,
But the caves are mysterious.

Jade Elizabeth Hodgson (10)
Bramley St Peter's CE Primary School

The Woman That Was As Fat As A Mat

The woman was as fat as a mat
She owned the fattest cat
The cat got hit by two cars
And shot up to Mars
It never came back down that poor cat
The owner was as flat as a mat
She's very, very weird
She's growing a big beard
The woman, the woman, the woman was as flat as a mat
One day the woman lay in a pool
She was trying to be so cool
And then she was thinking of drawing a den
With the most colourful pen
Then the fat cat
Landed on the woman that was as flat as a mat
Then the woman jumped in joy
And said, 'Hooray, you're a good boy!'

Aaron Woolner (9)
Bramley St Peter's CE Primary School

The Blue Screen

On the blue screen, on the blue screen,
What will you see?

On the blue screen we go to the beach,
The sand is so, so soft like a pillow,
Wearing sunglasses we look as cool as Mr Freeze.
On the blue screen we go to Coronation Street,
Where people fight like lions,
But it's only acting.
On the blue screen we go skydiving,
We are flying like an aeroplane,
The fluffy clouds going in your face.

Alex Cairns (10)
Bramley St Peter's CE Primary School

There's A Peter Griffen On The Street

There's a Peter Griffen on the street,
He's trying to find a bite to eat.
He trashes things here to there,
He doesn't like things very fair.
He's a very mean dude,
He's not very cool,
He's a very . . .
He's a very . . .
He's a very grumpy man.
So if Peter comes to you,
I think you should hit him with a shoe.
He's a very mean dude,
He's not very cool,
He's a very . ..
He's a very . . .
He's a very grumpy man.

Kane Preskey (11)
Bramley St Peter's CE Primary School

There's A Monster In Our School

There's a monster in our school
And only I know he plays pool.
He acts as if he's cool
There's a monster in our school.
He thinks he's really great,
His head's a funny shape,
It looks like a grape.
He sits in the gym
Thinking he's the king,
But I know he can't sing.
He thinks he's really cool,
His head's a funny shape,
And it looks like a grape.
He supports Leeds United,
And I know he's short-sighted,
But he still thinks he's cool,
Oh my gosh, there's a monster in the school.

Josh Fink (10)
Bramley St Peter's CE Primary School

Love

Love is like beautiful roses,
Like they're sitting next to poses.
Love's always there to stop
The bunny making me want to hop.

Love is great, it never goes away,
It just makes you want to say hooray.
Hooray, hooray, it never goes away,
Hooray, hooray, it never goes away.

Love makes you happy,
When your chappy
Helps you out.

Love is great, it never goes away,
It just makes you want to say hooray.
Hooray, hooray, it never goes away,
Hooray, hooray, it never goes away.

Emily Humphreys (9)
Bramley St Peter's CE Primary School

The Chilling Cave

Entering the cave, the chilling cave,
Feeling the cold, strong, rocky stalactites,
As sharp as Dracula's fangs.

Entering the cave, the chilling cave,
Hearing the water dripping,
Telling me its story like a whispered opera.

Entering the cave, the chilling cave,
From the light powering the world,
To the darkness as dark as a starless night.

Leaving the cave, the chilling cave,
From the light to dark and dark to light,
So this is goodbye chilling cave.

Lee McGill (10)
Bramley St Peter's CE Primary School

Extremely Milked Over Walk

The birds flew in the air with leaves on the floor
Where? There. Where? There. Where? Actually there.
The walking boots giving people blisters
Like your foot is on fire like a melting marshmallow,
The stinking of the cows munching their food.
Where? There. Where? There. Where? Actually there.
The smell of the original cow poo, yuck, yuck,
The sheep that smell.
Where? There. Where? There. Where? Actually there.
The grass looks like the sea, it is cold and wet,
Small gaps to get through.
Where? There. Where? There. Where? Actually there.
The sun will rise, darkness will drop,
Where? There, Where? There. Where? Actually there.
I love it, I love it, I'm happy.
The slime of the rocks and on the rocks the shine from the sun.

Cameron Brown (10)
Bramley St Peter's CE Primary School

The Blue Screen

On the blue screen I saw myself,
On the beach the sand was like a pillow,
Water was white as snow from the foam.

On the blue screen I was in the Stone Age with the dinosaurs,
I saw cave men invent fire,
The cave men were running from dinosaurs.

On the blue screen I was skydiving out of an aeroplane,
Like a bird flying in the breeze,
The fluffy clouds flew in my face.

On the blue screen I was a weather man,
Predicting the rain, snow, sun, wind,
That was exciting,
Sometimes I got it wrong and people got angry with me.

On the blue screen I had an adventure.

Adam Georgeson (10)
Bramley St Peter's CE Primary School

There's A Monster In Our School

There's a monster in our school
but I know he's there, I'm not a fool
He lives in the staff room
for anyone that goes in there it is certain doom.

So . . .

If you leave him alone
and just wander home
it won't make him mad
so in the morning he won't be bad.

Chewing up doors
and ripping up floors
but really he's not all bad
actually he's my dad.

Bradley Lewis Jack Marfitt (10)
Bramley St Peter's CE Primary School

The Blue Screen

Amazingly I went on the blue screen,
Firstly I went on the Stone Age,
Cave men were inventing fire,
Bright green dinosaurs chased me like headless chickens.

I went to Bradford Museum,
It was extremely awesome,
My favourite thing was the blue screen,
It was the best time ever!

Secondly I went skydiving,
I was zooming across the city like an aeroplane.

I went to Bradford Museum,
It was extremely awesome.
My favourite thing was the blue screen,
It was the best time ever!

Jared Blake (10)
Bramley St Peter's CE Primary School

Caving

Walking into the deep dark cave
It was pitch-black
Until I turned my light on.

The walls were damp
And cold and hard
Rocks surrounding me.

The water dripping
Like a tap
Water washing from nowhere.

When we came out
There was fresh grass
Fresh air through my nostrils
I had fun in the caves.

Lily Hunter (10)
Bramley St Peter's CE Primary School

Hallowe'en

I love Hallowe'en
and I love that scene
on Hallowe'en night
I have a fright
hopefully in the morning it will be alright

On Hallowe'en night
I give everybody a fright
and I will be coming tonight . . .

At night in the dark
I see ghosts and vampires
waiting for children

On Hallowe'en night
I give everybody a fright
and I will be coming tonight.

Adam Harron (10)
Bramley St Peter's CE Primary School

Heavenly Lime

A slice of Heaven glimmering in the sunlight,
Emerald treasured liquid passing through,
It gleams and glitters with a burst of hynotising flavours.
A spoonful of lime, an obstacle cloak wrapped around
like a sheet of armour protecting as princess.
The cloak is unwrapped and leaks a cascading waterfall
with an esteemed sight, and a pleasant aroma.
The gem invades the air with a paradise of dancing flavours.
The scent lasts as the jade green stone slithers down
sending out attractive shoots of silky emerald flavours
like a lime river passing through the mouth.
The luxurious gem explodes and slithers away into a midnight
ball of darkness and moonlight
and finally disappears never to be seen again.

Sophie Metcalfe (10)
Churwell Primary School

Mysterious Gem

As purple as a jewel,
Or an ancient pebble from the sea.
A piece fallen from a lost crown,
That has never been found.

Just like a delicately perfumed fruit,
A citrus aroma will engulf you,
With the most wondrous scent.

It's got a protective crystalline,
It's so rock-hard nothing can get through,
A jewel waiting to leap out of its treasure chest,
But one day the barrier will break.

Suddenly it erupts with flavours,
Like an endless river of wonder,
Then it descends into a waterfall,
With exploding fireworks in your mouth,
And then no more.

Georgia Wilson (11)
Churwell Primary School

Heavenly Gem

As pink as a luscious cherry's cheek sunbathing in its paradise city
Pearl pink streams flow around the miniature town.

The transparent clear mantle patiently waiting to be unwrapped
The tarnished unyielding, transparent armour fits firmly.

A wondrous aroma of strawberry goodness invades your nostrils
The wonderful perfumed sensation is locked in your nose forever.

A protective, bumpy crystalline barrier will hold it forever
As immense as a muscular rugby player holds a ball in a match.

A mountain of flavours erupt on your tongue
The appetizing taste tingles your tastebuds and stays in your mouth forever.

Elizabeth Earnshaw (10)
Churwell Primary School

The Emerald Sherbet

An emerald green tablet smooth and bouncy
covered in a transparent mantle glimmering in the sun.
An emerald grasshopper pouncing in grass that is golden,
exploring the open.
A transparent mantle holding the emerald tight and clean
from the rain.
The emerald warrior swipes his mantle off his back looking
at the paradise in front of him.
A glossy impenetrable warrior waiting for this moment
to happen, then *boom!*
The barrier is no more.
A tingly flavour bursts out covering the hole
with a coat of melon.
The warrior struggles to swallow the emerald slime
because it's so dense and ancient.
The pearl-white army crunches and swallows the slime emerald
in one and no more . ..

Connor James Ridgeway (10)
Churwell Primary School

Fruit Sherbet

The big roaring tiger bright as the sun
is trying to get past the sharp spiky ghost army
The attractive tiger is trying to burst open the crystal clear cave
tunnels through the skinned lines
The charming smell of fresh orange
A perfume smell for whoever's got a lucky chance to eat on it
The fine orange-coloured beach ball slips into someone's
round red circled mouth
The tiger goes down a long silky tube
The sugary tiger bursts open with orange you've
never seen before
The gold runs away and finishes its life
Down in a deep dark cabinet.

Aidan Sheard (10)
Churwell Primary School

Fruit And Sherbet

As violet as a shiny violet gem,
A miniature dinosaur egg,
Seems like a mystical gemstone,
The amazing wizard's locket of magical spells.

It smells of strawberry jelly,
A wonderful minty smell swimming up your nostrils,
The sweetness, *ahh,* the sweetness.

The feeling you get when you feel it so crunchy,
Smooth as an elastic ball,
A rock as hard as a brick.

The fabulous taste,
It's like eating a slice of Heaven,
Or maybe some children having a snowball fight,
Possibly as an almighty strike on your tongue,
A mouth-watering sensation.

Aimee McLaren (11)
Churwell Primary School

Untitled

A soft sticky lime atomic crystal bursting
out of your crumbling mind,
leathered with luxurious valuables coating
with an impenetrable scent of lime,
A charming delightful obstruction created on a palisade,
we've never seen the palisade.
The ancient announcement, we reveal a new unyielding scent,
of the luxurious green aroma,
of the Mediterranean Sea,
Oh no the gem's broken,
The end of the gem we see,
my heart's now broken,
I may live without thee.

Zak Haimid (10)
Churwell Primary School

A Heavenly Surprise

A long lost dazzling diamond as red as blood, crying out
to be freed from the battlefield.
The war has been won, the warrior picks up its prey . . .

He opens the crystalline barrier and is enticed by its inflexibility.
The warrior walks towards the treasure chest of unwanted
goods and the barrier is no more . . .

The warrior lifts the gem to his nostrils and inhales
the inviting aroma.
He tries to stop himself but he cannot resist the temptation . . .

He places the gem into his mouth, a cavern guarded
by wondrous white soldiers and . . . *crunch!*
A waterfall of flavours cascades down his throat
And the gem is no more.
Even though the gem has been devoured there is still
an endless river of flavour in the warrior's mouth.

Daniel Luke Caulfield (10)
Churwell Primary School

Rubylicious

It's an endless cascading waterfall
A long-lost fallen piece of a twinkling amethyst that glows
in the midnight sky
A polished gem glistening from a dilapidated crown
The protective crystalline barrier is the armour of the gemstone
The wrapper is exposed while tossed about
The precious stone has a glowing smile
The sweet aroma fills the air with the smell of a perfumed bursting
fragrance that hypnotises any admirer
It's a miniature world inside my mouth
The gem is now crushed in pieces of treasured sherbets
A strawberry paradise Heaven of an appetising sensation
It falls . . . falls till it's gone.

Olivia Swaine (11)
Churwell Primary School

The Sombre Fruit Sherbet

A glistening piece of amber,
Enveloped in a crystalline barricade,
Sitting sombrely in a daze of thought,
Waiting for his dream.
His dream eventually came true when a freedom fighter came along,
He freed the gem from his celluloid prison,
Unleashing his hypnotic Clementine scented gas,
His icy confinement thrown away,
Unveiling a priceless stone.
The freedom fighter, mesmerised, pushed the amber to his soft lips,
Opened his mouth and popped it in.
Pearl-white warriors attacked with full force,
As an explosion of sweet and sour took over his mouth.
The gemstone has gone,
All is lost.

Daniel Brown (10)
Churwell Primary School

The Emerald Explosion

A shimmering emerald pearl winking in the moonlit sky,
Waiting impatiently, protected by its impenetrable mantle,
A glimpse of a knight absconding from the room next door,
Hiking towards the luxurious pearl, showing no fear,
Closer and closer to the dancing pearl he gets,
The fearless silk silver mantle lunged to its ambitious death,
Revealing a remarkable kind king,
Letting off a despising beautiful fragrance,
Looking at the knight with a captivating aspect,
But the knight showing no guilt,
The pearl looking urgent for its waited moment.
As the knight is attacking the pearl, the white shield goes
Into the pearl making a stream of red love,
The buds applauding the excitement,
And finally, no more.

Luke Ambler (10)
Churwell Primary School

Paradise Of Heaven

As yellow as a sunflower, the topaz gem in a ray
of blinding sunlight.
A petal of a daffodil floating around the world in the breeze.
Covered from head to foot with a dazzling crystalline
piece of armour.
The glistening topaz gem squeezes its beautiful golden body
and shakes off its protective layer to reveal . . .
A treasured long lost gem with veins of sour sugary powder.
Suddenly it gets popped into a rushing flow of sticky mess
on a scorching red river.
The sour sugary powder dissolves into a massive flow
of sourness.
And gets tinier and tinier by the minute.
Finally . . . nothing is left but the distant sensation of pleasure.

Claire Lister (11)
Churwell Primary School

Sizzling Sensation

An orange fire-coloured jewel sits below the burning red sun.
It is protected by blazing coloured crystals which surround
the priceless jewel.
The crystalline coat reveals a precious gem which has
the appearance of a stripy tiger.
The aroma of a fresh orange slowly dissolves into the air.
The special person is lured by the fragrance of the fresh
oranges in the air.
As quick as a flash the stripy gemstone disappears
to an unknown cavern, guarded by a diamond army.
Slowly the jewel dissolves in the cavern and then a citrus blast
of the freshest oranges in the land explode like an explosion
of fireworks and then . . . it is gone.

Josh Falkiner (10)
Churwell Primary School

The Charming Jewel

A charming purple crystal jewel,
The polished jewel with a pathway going to Heaven,
The sparkling jewel staring at you, the veins are attractive to you,
In the delightful crystalline case waiting for it to come out,
The giant comes to the fine gem,
He rips the crunchy wrapper off the gem,
The charming purple crystal jewel comes out,
It smells like blackcurrant perfume,
In a second he puts it in his mouth, the gem is all crunchy,
That is delightful,
I need another,
No more left.

Caitlan Sharp (11)
Churwell Primary School

Flavour Of Wonder

A treasured jewel that shines in the morning sun.
A mouth-watering gem with an explosion of flavours,
waiting to erupt.
A cascading waterfall with an endless river of wonder.
A protective crystalline barrier cuddles it with a hypnotizing
flavour guarding it.
A piece of enchanting sun locked in a priceless kingdom
full of dazzling gems.
An ancient gemstone with bursting flavours is sliding down,
down into the bottomless pit.
Then a *crack!*
An explosion of flavour is left as evidence.

Abbie Woodley (11)
Churwell Primary School

The Story Of A Sweet

An emerald gem blinking in the sun,
Waiting for a mysterious moving figure,
The transparent stockade ready to be taken away.
Then in one sudden movement the clear obstruction is no more,
A gemstone is removed and a lime aroma pervades the air,
The tall object seemed to love the scent.
In one sudden movement the object had disappeared into a dark wet cave.

A gleaming white army protecting the exit,
A sudden strike cracks the unyielding surface,
The burst of flavours are like lemons and apples
And all at once it disappears.

Thomas Chadwick (10)
Churwell Primary School

The Ruby Sweet!

A shimmering ruby glints in the sun,
cowering in its tightly concealed and defensive cloak
as the sly warrior creeps cautiously towards the enchanting
magenta jewel twinkling attractively.
When the finger touches it a luxurious cherry fragrance fills
the air causing a hand to viciously grasp the barrier and peel it
off to reveal a mystical gem glittering like a star . . .
until the ruby is roughly forced into a midnight cave.
An army of crystals cut through the strong but defeated gem.
A burst of sherbet and with a final grind,
No more . . .

Rebecca Firth (11)
Churwell Primary School

The Gleaming Orange Gem

An esteemed slice of Heaven,
A golden line embroidered gem glints in the dazzling sun.
The transparent impenetrable shield protects the glossy, taste
tingling gem.
The keen warrior collects the gem cautiously and tears the shield off.
With its rich, luscious, fruity scent it clouds the air.
It hypnotises the warrior with its gorgeous scent.
The gem is dropped into a battlefield with pristine soldiers guarding.
The warrior tastes a burst of cascading waterfall.
The gem is battled to its death
And the gem is no more!

Aman Bassi (11)
Churwell Primary School

Sherbet Delight

A blood-red polished ruby comforted by a transparent force field,
With dark blood veins streaming through the impenetrable jewel.
A crystal clear army ready to attack any incoming competition.
The unknown warrior heading towards the firm gemstone,
A cherry aroma enters the air and the scent controls any
person's mind.
The warrior is drawn towards the charming sweet,
He unravels the crystal cape and a sweet smell enters the air,
A clear crystal army stops the warrior.
A tongue-tingling taste, a fruity *explosion,*
Gulp, gulp and no more . . .

Aimee Hawkins (10)
Churwell Primary School

Mysterious Gem

A golden tiger from a long lost world
A sapphire gem from an erupting volcano
As orange as the sun, the gem glistening miles away
The crystalline cloak reveals the gem
The mouth-watering aroma attacks my senses
The phenomenal explosion of flavours invades my nostrils
The decrepit darkness surrounds the mouth-watering mystical world
A cascading waterfall leads me to a world of wonder
Just like a slice of Heaven
I am left bewildered.

Ravi Patel (10)
Churwell Primary School

The Ruby Gem

A polished sweet ruby red gem winking and glistening in the sunlight,
With its scarlet poison of juice,
As it lays there on the bumpy rough surface.
Waiting to be swept away by a big paw of a fierce beast,
The crystal clear cloak tied all the way around
Is finally thrown back and no more of the cloak.
It lands on a pink spongy surface,
Crunch! The sherbet flavour bursts out with even more surprise
And *gulp*, it falls down a deep dark hole
And . . . no more!

Abigail Ryatt (10)
Churwell Primary School

A Fruit Sherbet

A crystal gem waiting for someone to consume it.
The gemstone is covered in a cape of glass,
The wrapper is thrown off by a warrior of gold,
Dear gem smells like a fresh new bottle of perfume,
The fine gem disappears into the cavern of the warrior
And no more . . .
The warrior's tongue is tingling like a bee just stung it,
The gem has melted,
A sherbet explosion,
Gone . . .

Libby Faye Millard (10)
Churwell Primary School

Untitled

As yellow as a fallen piece of enchanting sun
from a microscopic world.
The gem is as shiny as topaz from an esteemed crown.
Under its layers of crystalline armour an unyielding crystal
is revealed.
A citrus gasp invades all
And an aroma of lemon hypnotises everyone with its scent.
The priceless stone gets plunged into a fast flowing red river.
An eruption starts and a sour powder slithers down to an
unknown world with the crushed rock never to be found again.

Chloe Ely (10)
Churwell Primary School

Sweet Emerald

A green gem barricaded by an enshrouded mantle
The gem was to be consumed
A perplexing warrior traipsed to the green gem
Suddenly the warrior shredded the mantle off!
Its beauty was revealed . . .
The warrior reached for the crystalised gem
When all was quiet the green emerald entered the
pearl-guarded tunnel
The warrior's mouth had an explosion of flavours
Next, all was quiet . . .

Thomas Smith (10)
Churwell Primary School

The Topaz King

The Topaz King sits on the flat surface wearing a crystalline coat,
As the giant slips it off, the air turns into a citrus gas,
The coat floats into a treasure chest full of wasted goods.
The revealed king becomes a gemstone full of fast flowing veins,
Gushing with the blood of gods.
Suddenly he is airborne, landing on a damp red river.
No sooner than he has arrived he is being devoured by waves of
sticky liquid.
Now his veins burst, setting free the delicious blood.
This will be the end of the king.

Aaron Cawood (10)
Churwell Primary School

The Death Of A Sweet

A radiant jewel glittering in the vibrant sun,
Waiting for an unexpected visit by a warrior,
With its impenetrable defences the jewel will remain secure.
Suddenly the jewel is under attack,
The warrior bursts through the barrier to find . . .
An untouched jewel with a citrus aroma.
The warrior hurls the jewel into an unilluminated cavern
Where it is comforted by a pink snake before white boulders
Cascade onto the jewel and devour it
And no more.

Luke Gough (10)
Churwell Primary School

Warrior Of Gold

I am a gem attracting all with my plump body of gold,
I am a rocky red moon protected by a crystal clear atmosphere,
There is a hooded figure on the prowl,
Suddenly he attacks and the atmosphere is sucked away!
I helplessly try defensive tactics, a strong, over-powering aroma,
It's not working!
I am a fiery orange ant, victim of the smooth, snowy-white pistons,
Crush! Stomp! Crush! Stomp!
When will it end?
I am a slithering embryo falling hopelessly into a dark,damp cavern.

Cameron Rhodes Williams (11)
Churwell Primary School

Man Vs Sweet

Abandoned for many years,
The gem lies alone,
Waiting for the unknown warrior
To peel back the winking hood
And reveal the glossy unruffled coat,
A citrus aroma fills the air,
But then the jewel is uncovered
To an army of pearl-white soldiers,
Into battle it goes in an unilluminated cavern,
Until no more.

Adam Caulfield (10)
Churwell Primary School

The Emerald Lime Sweet

A giant emerald sweet waiting for its moment,
The crystalline shield protecting the banging in the duel,
Being torn to bits the scent of lime is established,
The beautiful lime aroma is tempting the hand towards it,
Finally the duel has reached the cave,
And then *chomp, chomp, chomp,*
It is falling down the pipe and then,
Down in the dump,
Burp!
The scent is let back out!

Jack Atkinson (10)
Churwell Primary School

The Dream Sweet

As purple as a flower, as luscious as a cherry.
A precious stone from the depths of a golden tomb
in a long lost forgotten city.

The crackling crystalline cloak protects the treasured gemstone
until it slips away and reveals the magic within.

A wonderful burst of fragrance invades my senses.

An endless river of wonder that explodes
like a cascading firework.

Toni Rodgers (10)
Churwell Primary School

Fruit Sherbet

A priceless red ruby from the precious jewelled encrusted crown
of the queen of Egypt
It glistens like a sparkling star in the sky behind
its protective cloak
It feels smooth like a washed-up pebble on the sand
A burst of hypnotizing flavours invades my nostrils
Then, unleased from its hardened exterior comes an explosion
of flavours like an endless river of wonder
The sharp tangy sensation fizzes until there is no more.

Alex Cunningham (10)
Churwell Primary School

Sherbet Of The Stars

A golden tiger waiting to catch its prey
But starts to run as he sees a hunter.
Its crystalline obstruction saves the day
That doesn't last long as it gets unraveled.
It discharged a lemon and lime fragrance
Which the hunter could not nit fall for.
The shining tiger finally gets killed and eaten.
But it explodes like a firework, 100 bangs per crunch.
And then . . . it is gone.

George Barrass (10)
Churwell Primary School

Sweet Citrus

A pure citrus gem from an ancient world,
Sparkling in the sunlight in its silver cloak,
When suddenly the cloak is ripped off.
The sweet aroma is released,
Everything is still.
Suddenly it disappears in a dark tunnel guarded
by a pearl-white army,
Smash! The gem is crushed
And is no more.

Georgina Metcalf (10)
Churwell Primary School

Purple Emerald

A smooth purple emerald orb smothered in purple and pink
motorway paths in a crystal clear concealed cape available
to be peeled.
The crystal clear concealed cape peeled off.
Now the smooth shiny orb's thick coating makes your mouth
water in delight.

Josh Dixon (10)
Churwell Primary School

Emerald Ivy

A precious emerald jewel from a long forgotten crown.
It glistens and gleams from behind its crystalline protective
cape waiting to be unveiled.
Slowly the silken cape falls away revealing
an unexpected treasure.
The citrus aroma tantalises your senses as its fruitness explodes
with a burst of acid sourness.
Like a cascading waterfall it falls . . . falls . . . until . . . it has gone.

Kelly-Beth Marais (10)
Churwell Primary School

Sherbet Delight

An emerald-green sparkling gem sitting in a protective
crackling crystalline coat waiting to be unveiled.
A blast of fruit flavours leak through its vessels.
It cries out for survival in a silent tunnel.
Anxiously the emerald gem rapidly pumps green blood!
Squirting everywhere.
The guarded barrier suddenly bursts out sour showers
and erupting flavours of colours.

Ross Kavanagh (10)
Churwell Primary School

Mysterious Gem

As green as grass, the dazzling emerald is secretly hidden
in the anonymous meadow.
The glistening gem is surrounded by a protective crystalline
barrier that takes you to another world.
A sweet smelling aroma invades your nostrils as the precious
gem loses its lime blood as it's devoured.
As a burst of sour showers from the crushed jewel slither
down . . . down . . . down . . . gone.

Harry Shelborn (10)
Churwell Primary School

The Glistening Lemon Jewel

The crystal clear wrapper glistened in the sunlight,
The only obstacle shielding a golden jewel.
I couldn't resist, I unveiled the delightful treat,
A sweet sensation with a zesty aroma,
I was drawn to the fine delight.
Suddenly it disappeared into a dark unknown cavern.
A blast of flavours tingled my tastebuds and there was no more!

Isha Komeh (10)
Churwell Primary School

A Fruity Explosion

A delightful sweet which explodes
With enjoyable, fruity, charismatic flavour,
To try and break through the barrier,
A sweet with tunnels, stripes,
A ruby of redness polished till it gleams,
And it's gone *mmm* . . . scrumdidlyumcious.

Harrison Armitage (10)
Churwell Primary School

Sibling Rivalry

On the Savannah sand
A pride of lions on the prowl
Only active at dusk
But a secret is untold

The pride leader
Starts his patrols
But on a cliff top
A more sinister rival appears

On a cliff top
Far away
The mysterious shadow watches
His eyes are filled with flames of fury

As the leader is asleep
The figure unveils himself
A lion who dreams of being king
His coat dark like his heart

As he creeps up behind him
His claws like razors
His eyes like lasers
His teeth like the edge of a blade

One quick bite to the throat
A silent assassin the figure was
The lion now rules over the pride
The lions cry out in despair

Their cries echo through time and space
Doomed for all eternity
His power is rising
But the rivals are rising as well . . .

Aaron Adams (10)
Grove Lea Primary School

A Life Of Colours

My life is a sea full of bright luminous colours.
Pink - girls and pigs are totally different but are both pink.
Green - nature is the green in my life which reflects
off the green emeralds I treasure.
Red - red represents the two favourite fruits I love
and the fire in a red ruby.
Yellow - the gleaming sun that shines and the loud scary
thunder are different to the yellow smiley face I wear at school.
Blue - the blue in my life is the deep blue sea
which is home to all sea creatures and the sky
which is a playground to birds.
Black and white - the black and white in my life is a proud
spotty Dalmatian, my favourite dog of all.
These are the bright colours of my life.

Jay Hedley (10)
Horbury Primary School

A Life Of Colours

I am from a world filled with different colours,
From the pinky, purple make-up on Saturday night,
To the boring burgundy of school.
I am from a world spotted with fluorescent yellow -
To help me in the dark,
To the dark, murky swamp.
I am the black and white pieces of the chessboard,
To the mellow amber of the sun.
I am from a world sprinkled with fizzy orange fireworks,
To the glistening white of the lily,
I am the bright red of my house team,
To the turquoise of my favourite colour.
This is the rainbow of my life, spotted and sprinkled
With different colours.

Alexandra Hepplewhite (10)
Horbury Primary School

A Life Of Colours

This is my life,
My life is full of extraordinary colours,
It brings colour into the world . . .

I am the changing colours of the sea,
I am the transparent of the skeleton fish,
I am the bright red of the big bold squid,
I am the bold grey of the mighty vicious shark,
I am the tiny pink prawns which swim about the coral reef,
I am the orange sea horse slowly wriggling away,
I am the sapphire blue of the giant blue whale,
I am the shining pink jellyfish,
I am the brilliant silver of the darting sardines . . .
These are my colours of the deep blue-green sea.

Aaron Dolan (10)
Horbury Primary School

A Life Of Colours

I am the paint palette that mixes together
and brings colour into my life.
I am the light pink in my cheeks when I'm with my friends.
I am the burgundy of my uniform that I am proud to wear.
I am the emerald-green that marks my date of birth
and rings a bell to all my family.
I am the bright yellow that fills my family with joy
and brings us all together.
I am the luscious red that fills my heart with passion.
I am the scruffy white that fills me with joy and laughter
as my dog runs around me.
These are my colours that paint my life
and these are just a few of them.

Jessica Norfolk (10)
Horbury Primary School

A Life Of Colours

I am made of colours, my life is colours.
I am a yellow shine of happiness when I see someone special.
I am a cool blue in the morning and by evening I am deeply
dark with tiredness.
My cheeks are pink from the goldness of laughter.
From the time of gloomy grey, brown and black,
to the rainbows of day.
I am the black of darkness of night and I am the magical sunrise
of the morning.
I am the thorny red rose from sadness, disgust
and disappointment.
I'm made of colour, my life is colours.

Kate Atkinson (10)
Horbury Primary School

A Life Of Colours

I am from a world of bright colours,
From the sunny yellow banana - my favorite fruit.
I am from the sparkling orange fireworks that fly through
the jet-black sky at night.
I am from the crystal blue of clear, calm water where the wild
animals come to drink and relax.
I am from the burgundy red tomato ketchup -
my favourite sauce.
I am from the dark blue carpet in the playroom in my house.
I am from the bright green of plants and nature
that surround me.
This is my world of colours and I do not wish to change it.

Thomas Wilson (10)
Horbury Primary School

A Life Of Colours

I am from a world with colours bright,
From the light of the day to the dark of the night.
The purple of grapes, my favourite fruit,
To the white of Leeds, my favourite team.
The clear blue of Caribbean waters,
Where I go from time to time.
From the red of anger I sometimes get,
To the orange of my belt on a Friday night.
From the happiness green on a Saturday morning,
To the black of sadness on a Monday morning.
These are the colours that fill my life,
How I would be sad without them.

Sam Mandi-Ghomi (10)
Horbury Primary School

A Life Of Colours

I am from a world of colour,
I am the clear blue in the sky,
I am the mucky white on a football,
I am the juicy red in strawberries,
I am the bright green in the limes,
I am the deep purple in the blackberries,
I am the blushing pink in my cheeks,
I am the starry yellow in the lemons,
I am the creamy brown inside a conker,
I am the deep blue in the sea,
I am the rich burgundy on my school hoody,
I am everywhere and in everyone.

Levi Goodridge (11)
Horbury Primary School

A Life Of Colours

The world is made of colours
The grass is bright green
The still deep water is blue
Your emotions are made of colours
Dark red brings anger
Smoky black brings sadness to the world
Amber is happy and joyful
Colours are on your food
Like the bright red on the juicy water melon
The bright yellow pineapple
And the bright green grapes
This is my life of colours.

Harry John Lindley (10)
Horbury Primary School

A Life Of Colours

The world is a colourful place
The world has lots of chocolate brown branches
where the amber autumn leaves lie just waiting to fall
And those amber leaves fly round the blueberry blue
and lime green world
The world is a colourful place
So the amber leaves pass by the gruesome, deathly
black graveyard
The world is a colourful place
See the amber leaves soaring over the white
and the dinky pink rose also the sparkly blue water
The world is a colourful place.

Georgina Vaile (10)
Horbury Primary School

A Life Of Colours

This is my life of colours.
I am blue on Monday morning,
I am orange on the warm weekends,
I am burgundy in the week,
I am pink when I play and laugh,
From dull grey deaths,
To lovely colourful births.
I am red when I get into my warm bed,
I am the colour of food,
I am the colour of giant rainbows,
I am the emerald green giving a glint of jealousy.
This is my life in high definition.

Jack Watson (10)
Horbury Primary School

A Life Of Colour

Colours here, colours there,
Colours here, there and everywhere.
I am steaming grey when I am moody mad,
To jet-black of upsetting death.
I am full of funny pink when I am happy.
The world is full of colour.
I am blue when I am sad,
To rosy-red when I am embarrassed,
To pongy purple when I am sleepy.
Our world is full with colour,
That's what makes our world interesting.

Zoe Jones (10)
Horbury Primary School

A Life Of Colours

This is the window of life
I am the grey, the blue and the bright
I am the red and the blue together
From the red of anger
To the deep blue of the sea
I am the bright white of the moon
And the shining yellow of the sun
I am the orange in lava
And the black of night
This is the rainbow
Painted by life.

Finley Marshall (10)
Horbury Primary School

A Life Of Colours

This is my colourful life.
When I am green, I feel really mean.
When I am red, I'm real mad.
When I am yellow, I'm mellow.
When I am purple, I am relaxed.
When I am orange, I am warm.
When I am blue, I am cold.
When I am white, I will have had a fright.
When I am brown, I feel down.
When I am pink, I am embarrassed.
This is my life in fast moving colour.

Jessica Downing (10)
Horbury Primary School

A Life Of Colours

As I run through the autumn leaves,
The brown and orange colours float swiftly down from the trees.
I look back and giggle with my friends and study the tracks we make.
I take off my muddy black shoes and scoop out the mud
And leaves from my shoes.
The day ends and I put on my black shoes.
I step in a muddy brown puddle.
I race to the blue car.
I get changed out of my burgundy uniform
And into my red and grey clothes.
This is a day in my life of colours.

Benjamin Hant (10)
Horbury Primary School

A Life Of Colours

This is the world I live in that is full of bright and dull,
I am the dark grey shadows walking in the misty woods,
staring at all of the dull colours.
I am the joyful spring green, before I change to the crispy,
white, cold winter.
I am the aqua blue sea chasing surfboarders back to shore.
I am the black ruined cave of the fierce, grizzly bear.
I am the bright yellow sun smiling happily
at the rainbow-coloured Earth.
This is the world, no one can change it.

Robert Garside (10)
Horbury Primary School

A Life Of Colours

I'm the burgundy of my uniform filled with laughter and sadness.
Colour here, colour there, colour comes everywhere.
Death comes with black bulging colour.
Newborn comes with fuchsia of the happy times of our lives.
I'm from a world full of colours everywhere you look,
Colours here, there it's going to last forever.
Teal is when I feel sad but light green makes me feel alive!
And silver of a great beginning.
Multicoloured makes me feel like a lot of passion,
In my life from changes.

Ellia Wright (11)
Horbury Primary School

A Life Of Colours

I am from a world sprinkled with colour,
From the bright neon that helps me be seen,
To the dark and musty colours on a Monday morning,
From the glistening of the poppy,
To the crystal white of the daisy,
I am the dizzy pink and purple of a Saturday night,
From the silver of the moonlight shining on the lakes,
To the blowing orange sun,
I am the fizzy yellow and ocean blue of Bonfire Night,
This is the rainbow of my life!

Bethan Newsome (11)
Horbury Primary School

A Life Of Colour

I am made of colours,
I am the pink rosy cheeks of when I get embarrassed,
I am the peach colour of my skin,
I am the burgundy colour of my school uniform,
I am how I feel blue when I have to get up on a Monday morning,
I am the look of the bright blue sky with the beaming yellow sun in it,
I am the emerald green giving you a glint of jealousy,
I am the thorny red rose of my raging anger,
My life is made of colours,
I am made of colours.

Ella Carlton (10)
Horbury Primary School

A Life Of Colour

My life is a colourful world,
I am the green in the swaying grass,
I am the red in the bricks of my house,
I am the emerald-green giving you a glint of jealousy,
I am the grey on a dull day,
I am the blue on a bright day,
I am the dark green in the Christmas tree,
I am the brown in the tasty chocolate,
I am the crystal blue in the cold sea,
My life is very, very colourful.

Nicholas Calderley (10)
Horbury Primary School

A Life Of Colours

I am the blue of the sky and the walls of my bedroom,
I am the orange of my happiness, my laughter, my love,
I am the pink of my cheeks and the mystery behind my grin,
I am the brown of the mud which clings to me and steals the boots from my feet,
I am the grassy green of nature and the majority of my wardrobe,
I am the burgundy of my uniform which I'm proud to be wearing,
I am the brown of the bundle of fur which completes my family,
I have a life full of colours; these are just a few of them.

Olive Chappell-Davies (11)
Horbury Primary School

A Life Of Colours

This is my life full with colours.
I am morning blue sky,
I am the little grey squirrel that sits on our fence,
I am the orange leaves falling from the sky in autumn,
I am the soft white snow in winter,
I am the green, green grass on our football pitch,
I am the clear blue ocean,
I am the muddy footprints on our doorstep,
I am the emerald green on a conker shell!

Spencer Norton (10)
Horbury Primary School

A Life Of Colours

I am the emerald gleam in my firework.
I am a sapphire in a shiny sea.
I am the red in a ruby rose.
I am the grey in a moonlight sensation.
I am black in a cat's pupil.
I am the orange in a majestic lion.

Peter Broadhead (10)
Horbury Primary School

A Life Of Colours

I am from a world of bright colours,
from the bright blueberry sky to the lime green grass below.
I am from the bulging red fire that burns in my soul when I'm angry,
to the multicolours of the flowers.
I am from the maroon uniform I wear in the week,
to the Christmas colours on the Christmas tree.
I am from the smoky black sky at night,
to the calm aqua marine oceans.
This is my life and it is full of colours.

Eleanor Parker (10)
Horbury Primary School

A Life Of Colours

C olours are important in life,
O range reminds me of Bonfire Night.
L ife is surrounded by colours,
O range reminds me of baked beans.
U nder the sky are many colours,
R ed is a sign of anger and hate and the
S ight of colours shows different emotions.
This is a life of colours,
My life of colours.

Joshua Davidson-Page (11)
Horbury Primary School

A Life Of Colours

I am the gold in the jeweller's shop.
I am the blue in the lake of life.
I am the purple of the juicy grape that I bite into.
I am the red of the fireworks.
I am the pink of the flowers dancing in the breeze.
I am the black from Hallowe'en.

Billy Holliday (10)
Horbury Primary School

A Life Of Colours

My life is full of colour,
When I feel green I am very mean,
When I feel red I am very angry,
When I feel pink I am very embarrassed,
When I am blue I feel very cool,
When I am brown I feel very down,
When I am yellow I am a little mellow,
When I am white I have had a fright,
This is my life, these are my colours.

Emily Deuchars-Taylor (10)
Horbury Primary School

A Life Of Colours

This is the juicy orange of the orange that I love to eat.
This is the bright yellow gleaming sun
That I sometimes love and sometimes hate.
This is the black and grey of a dim funeral.
This is the pink and yellow of a happy wedding.
This is the beautiful light blue of the sky.
This is the lovely white of the floating clouds.
I love all the colours in the world,
There are such a lot of them.

Emma Rogers (11)
Horbury Primary School

A Life Of Colours

I am a girl out of this world with colours.
Blue - I am as bored as an old oak tree, blowing in the wind.
Pink - I am as happy as a laughing clown of laughter.
Red - I am as bad as devil, black hearted.
Orange - I am as calm as autumn when the crispy leaves fall from
the tall trees.
Black - I am as angry as anything could ever be.
Green - I am as tired as the long green grass blowing in the wind.
I am a girl of moods mixed with colours.

Freya Amelia Wilson (10)
Horbury Primary School

A Life Of Colours

My life of colours are in my eye.
I am bright blue in the sky.
When I turn to blue sometimes,
I am sad or happy.
My bedroom will be blue soon.
My uniform is burgundy for my school,
But at home I wear blue.
The blue is like a raindrop coming down.
This is who I am and I am glad to be here in colour.

Meghan Holliday (10)
Horbury Primary School

A Life Of Colours

I am from a world rich with colour,
From the bold red of my football team,
I am the happy orange of the Saturday nights,
I am the green of Christmas morning,
I am the mellow yellow of satisfaction on a happy day,
I am the gloomy grey of Monday mornings,
I am the bright neon colours that help me to be seen,
This is the rainbow of my life!

Edward Furlong (11)
Horbury Primary School

A Life Of Colours

I am the burgundy girl with a purple bedroom.
I am a happy girl but blue when I see the first sight
of my school.
I am a blonde girl with burgundy shiny glasses.
I have a blue teddy with blue eyes.
I am a lovely pink colour with blue eyes.
I have a lovely house but it is bright white.
This is my life and these are my colours.

Abbie Crossley (10)
Horbury Primary School

A Life Of Colours

I am a small person with lots of colours.
I am white with the winter snow,
I am orange with the autumn leaves,
My friends can make me more and more colours,
They make me purple with laughter,
They make me blue with sadness,
They make me gold with excitement
And red with anger.

David Mark Dalton (10)
Horbury Primary School

A Life Of Colours

I am from a world bright with colours,
The green that reminds me of the football field that I play on
And the fields at the bottom of my street.
The dark burgundy and grey of my school uniform,
And the grey gloomy feeling on a Monday morning I get with it.
The dark black anger that runs in my adrenaline,
But these are my colours,
These are the colours of my life.

Patrick Lewis (10)
Horbury Primary School

A Life Of Colours

This is my life of colours,
I am the morning blue sky,
I am anger when I wear red in autumn,
I am the deep dark brown mud in the garden,
I am always feeling blue on Monday mornings,
I am a little topaz orange caterpillar on an old crunchy leaf,
I am the autumn leaves falling on the dark, cold, wet ground.
These are my bright and dull colours of my life.

Lucy Gostelow (10)
Horbury Primary School

A Life Of Colours

I am a young boy who is a mixture of many colours.
I have friends who make me go pink with laughter or blue and sad.
I can be the sun which shines through my window,
Or the black murky water that flows past my house.
I am the white cold igloo in my garden at winter,
I am the sweet green grass in the spring,
I am the glowing blue water in the swimming pool,
I am many colours but they are my life.

Jack Gilbert (10)
Horbury Primary School

A Life Of Colours

Red - the roses in gardens that smell so sweet.
Blue - the sky in the morning.
Pink - the happy times.
Yellow - the afternoon sun glowing in the sky.
Orange - the sort of fruit.
Indigo - the splot of ink on my book.
This is the rainbow of my life,
The colours that I live in.

Alix Allsop (10)
Horbury Primary School

A Life Of Colours

I am a burgundy girl with a purple bedroom.
I have a black and white dog with a cheeky smile.
I am a happy girl but blue on Monday mornings.
I am a brown-haired girl with purple glasses.
I have an orange teddy with green eyes.
I am grey as I go to school.
This is my colourful life, no one can change it.

Teri Larkin (11)
Horbury Primary School

A Life Full Of Colours

I am from a world full of bright colours,
From the big shivering blue planet - my favourite colour.
Sometimes I am happy with gushing electric colours in my face,
Sometimes I am full of anger but anger is raging red.
When I'm embarrassed my face turns emerald amber,
But when I'm sad I go to my blistering room full of blue colours.
These are the colours of my life.

Alex Reynolds (10)
Horbury Primary School

A Life Of Colours

Life is like a paint palette full of lots of colours,
I am the green colour like the bright green grass,
I am the blue of the deep blue sea,
I am the orange when the leaves fall off the trees,
I am the red when I laugh on a Sunday,
I am the colour black like a dull sad day.
This is my life and these are my colours.

Stacey Young (10)
Horbury Primary School

A Life Of Colours

I am from a world full of colour,
from a planet like a yellow melon, my favourite fruit.
Sometimes I am full of dark red anger.
Sometimes I am full of happiness with full of gushing colours
in my face.
When I am mad I can see my navy blue reflection in the mirror.
These are the colours of my life.

Cody Daniel Selby(10)
Horbury Primary School

Life Of Colours

I am from a world of bursting colours.
I am from a theatre of big red pirates.
I am from a gang of thugs wearing dark black smirks.
This is the smoking black anger brooding inside me.
I am a raging red bull waiting to be released.
I am an inner beast, black and bold.
These are the colours of my life.

Tom Miller (10)
Horbury Primary School

A Life Of Colours

Life is a rainbow full of colours,
I am a jolly red person but I am blue on Mondays,
I am the soft white snow in the winter,
I am the flowing green grass on the spring mornings,
I am the red laughter on a weekend but behind is the gloomy grey I get when I receive bad news,
This is my life and these are my colours.

Lucy Smith (10)
Horbury Primary School

A Life Of Colours

I am the white lie behind my cheeky smile.
I am red on a Friday night as I laugh my head off.
I am blue as I walk back into school.
I am the pink pride as I am doing the Christmas play.
I am emerald-green that makes me shine with jealousy.
I am the smoky black with anger bursting out of me.
These are my colours, this is my life.

Jordan Reed (10)
Horbury Primary School

A Life Of Colours

This is the black bug that looks like the leaves that fall down in the autumn days.
This is the red that reminds me of dangerous people fighting others.
This is the crystal bit of the ice that goes in the sparkling lemonade.
This is the huge green and brown tree that shines in the purple night.
I am the gold of the tinsel shivering in the light.
I am the glossy bells which sit on the tree at Christmas.
I am made of twinkling colours that make the world colourful.

James Ward (11)
Horbury Primary School

Ideas From My Paintbox

Today,
I have come to say,
Would you like to see,
My paintbox?

Blue are the rivers rushing by,
Then you sit by a tree and look at the sky,
The pool is so cool and a very light blue,
I enjoy these things, don't know about you.

Red is the roaring fire on Bonfire Night,
The flames dancing is such a sight.
Blush of your cheeks if you're shy,
When someone you like passes you by.

White is snow, very cold,
Don't throw snowballs so I'm told,
Hot chocolate when I go inside,
Then under the covers I go and hide.

Lana Agar (10)
Inglebrook School

Emotions

Happy is the colour yellow
Happy tastes like a sweet banana
Happy looks like the big yellow sun
Happy sounds like my brother laughing
Happy feels like a warm cuddle
Happy smells like a yellow daffodil.

Creativity is the colour lime green
Creativity feels like sticky glue
Creativity looks like a bright picture
Creativity tastes like a sweetened lime
Creativity sounds like an owl hooting
Creativity smells like freshly cut grass.

Holly Saul (10)
Inglebrook School

Ideas From My Paintbox

Today
I have come to see
My paintbox

Blue is a whale blowing out water
The ocean's stormy waves crashing into the rocks
Fresh water from the river
Clear sky on a warm sunny day

Red is a clown's nose ready to make you laugh
The glowing fire of burning wood
A gigantic balloon floating in the sky
The feathers of a parrot perched up high

Green is grass, freshly cut
Summer trees silky and soft
Crystal eyes looking everywhere
Apples so juicy and sweet.

Charles Peacock (11)
Inglebrook School

Spells

Put into a cauldron
Ten spiders' legs
A slice of mouldy bread
Four wolves' eyes
Stir them up with
The dew of a bum bum tree
Six drops of beetles' blood
While you stir
Say this spell
Spiders' legs
And mouldy bread
Make this dog croak like a frog
Put a drop of the magic brew on the tongue of a dog.

Charlotte Riley (10)
Inglebrook School

Emotions

Joy is . . .

The colour is bright pink
It tastes like chocolate
It smells like a sweet rose
It looks like a clear mountain stream
It sounds like a sweet song of a bird in the morning
It feels like my bed.

Scared is . . .

Scared is like the colour black
Scared tastes like mouldy cheese
Scared smells like a damp old room
Scared looks like a black tunnel never-ending
Scared sounds like a deep, long cry
Scared feels like you are all alone.

Rosie Marsh (10)
Inglebrook School

Autumn Song

Today is the day when autumn starts,
When leaves turn red then brown.
The children love to play in the leaves
As they come tumbling down.

Sometimes I go conker picking
At this time of year
And gathoring acorns for his store
I see the squirrel's fur.

Harvest time is here again
And apples hang on trees.
But sometimes they're not there
But blown away by the breeze.

Grace Peacock (8)
Inglebrook School

Emotions

Joy is . . .

Joy is the colour green
It tastes like sour sweets
It smells of beautiful flowers
It looks like a brightly coloured picture
It sounds like joyful birds singing
It feels like my dog licking my face.

Love is . . .

Love is the colour pink
Love tastes of chocolate treats
Love smells like scented candles
Love looks like a lovely rose
Love sounds like beautiful music
Love feels like a loving hug.

Caleb Jenkins(10)
Inglebrook School

Birds Of Autumn

Autumn time is coming,
Harvest is on its way.
All the little birdies
Are coming out to play.

They're eating all the berries
And dancing on the leaves,
And sitting on the branches
Of the big brown trees.

They're singing and they're chirping
All of the day.
But soon they'll be migrating
And running away.

Lucy Hewitt (9)
Inglebrook School

Emotions

Kindness is a warm orange
Kindness tastes of chocolate cake
Kindness smells like yellow primroses
Kindness looks like a teddy bear coming up to me
Kindness sounds like birds cheeping to me
Kindness feels like a love heart in my tummy.

Anger is mean red
Anger tastes like rotten eggs
Anger smells like saltwater
Anger looks like someone yelling at me
Anger sounds like a howling wolf
Anger feels like stones throbbing down my throat.

Antonia Casey (9)
Inglebrook School

Mixed Feelings

My joy colour is yellow
It feels like my rabbit licking my fingers
Joy tastes like a ruby red apple
The smell of joy is warm hot chocolate
It sounds like a group of birds singing
Joy looks like a beautiful painting.

Blue is the colour of sadness
It tastes like a sour lemon
Sadness looks like a building on fire
It sounds like children screaming
Sadness smells like sour milk
It feels like a great big hole inside you.

Amy Henderson (8)
Inglebrook School

Mixed Emotions

Kindness is light orange
Kindness tastes of hot chocolate
Kindness smells like newly cut grass
Kindness looks like a blue sky on a summer's day
Kindness sounds like trees swaying in the wind
Kindness feels like a hot water bottle.

Jealousy is dark red
Jealousy tastes of bitter lemons
Jealousy smells like burnt toast
Jealousy looks like a crashing car
Jealousy sounds like a loud scream
Jealousy feels like being alone in a dark cave.

Leah Dunderdale-Smith (10)
Inglebrook School

Feelings

Happy is light yellow
Happy tastes of bubbly lemonade
Happy smells like my daddy cooking
Happy looks like autumn
Happy sounds like someone singing
Happy feels like my baby brother hugging me

Excitement is the colour red
It tastes like my favourite fish and chips
It looks like a butterfly flapping around me
Excitement smells like my dad
It sounds like my mummy calling
It feels like my rabbit rubbing its fur on me.

Jordan Webster (9)
Inglebrook School

Mixed Feelings

Happiness is the colour yellow.
Happiness tastes like hot chocolate.
Happiness smells like roses.
Happiness looks like my family.
Happiness sounds like birds singing.
Happiness feels like my cosy bed.

Sadness is the colour light blue.
Sadness tastes like rotten eggs.
Sadness smells like rotten apples.
Sadness looks like a baby crying.
Sadness sounds like the slamming of a door.
Sadness feels like somebody punching you in the face.

Olivia Waddington (10)
Inglebrook School

September

S chool starts again
E verybody comes back to work
P laytimes are fun
T rees that are really nice
E vening starts getting dark
M any conkers fall off trees
B eginning of autumn
E ven I will be playing with my football
R unning outside to have some fun.

André Earnshaw (10)
Inglebrook School

Treasure

Cycling on my bike crunching through leaves,
Cycling on my bike I heave and heave.
Cycling on my bike past a conker;
I go back for that conker.

Lucy Satur (10)
Inglebrook School

Crossgates

Crossgates is an incredible place!
Going round and round the roundabout,
What a magnificent thing to do,
It's so exciting,
It makes you want to go to the *loo!*

Crossgates is an incredible place!
Cool Coe's is the best place in the world!
At making gorgeous, crispy fish and chips!
They're all you need to make a perfect meal.
Be careful 'cause when you start eating,
You'll never be able to stop.

Crossgates is an incredible place!
Manston Park is definitely ace!
Tennis courts, football pitches,
Lots of fun in their muddy ditches!
I bet you can't believe it's all in Manston Park!

Crossgates is an incredible place!
Go to gorgeous Greggs and . . .
Buy perfect pizza slices,
At very cheap prices!

Crossgates is an incredible place!
I think you get the picture,
I don't want to rub it in your face but,
Crossgates is an incredible place!

Adam Vickers (10)
Manston St James CE Primary School

On A Train At Crossgates Station

Waiting at the train station,
Looking out for a train,
Standing in the shelter,
Trying to avoid the rain.

Waiting at the train station,
Soaking wet through,
Waiting, waiting, waiting
Wondering what to do.

Yes! Here comes a train right now,
It's been a long, long while.
I've never been on a train before,
I can't do anything but smile.

I'm very, very nervous
Thank goodness the waiting's through.
It screeches to a halt
Looking shiny and brand new.

I'm getting on the train right now
On my way to Crossgates.
I cannot wait to get there
To go shopping with my mates!

I look out of the window
And see blurred scenes go by.
The rhythm of the train tracks makes me relax and sigh.

I feel a jerk, the train has stopped
I sit there for a while.
This has been the best day ever
All I've done is smile.

I can't wait to get off
To go shopping with my mates.
I cannot wait to go explore
The suburb of Crossgates!

Zoe Dawn Driver (10)
Manston St James CE Primary School

In The Park

Now it's winter in the park
And my feet step on fallen snow,
I wear my hat, my gloves and scarf
And when it's dark home I'll go.

I awake in the morning's cold
And go to the park and play, play, play!
Worn out snow boots are so old,
As I say goodbye to the silver snow on that winter's day.

Soon comes spring, the still, still air
And along the coast of the green, green grass
The new flowers begin to grow,
Flowers of all colours people take with care,
To make sure they don't get trampled as they grow row by row.

Children having lots of fun,
With the sun so incredibly hot
And caps are worn to protect us from the sun,
To help with summer's plot.

As spring begins to fade
And summer runs along,
Water fights begin to raid
And the weatherman's never wrong.

In the summer days with the golden sun,
Children play throughout the day,
Playing's never done
And running every way.

As summer days pass by,
With races and football going on,
With kites flying high
And so golden shone.

With a *crunch* of leaves
That fall from above
And come from autumn trees,
'Autumn's here,' people shout with love.

The life from spring, the leaves that grow,
The leaves become all dry,
Autumn comes everyone knows,
It goes in to winter's cry.

Molly McPaul (11)
Manston St James CE Primary School

Crossgates

If you live far away
Get on a train come here
But if you live on the coast
Why buy a ticket to come close
Or just boast.

If you live far away
Can't get good meat
Then pop into Wilson's for millions . . .
They're the best you can eat
You could go back for billions.

If you live far away
Don't have a park
Bounce on into Manston Park
It's a good place to walk your dog
But don't go in the dark.

If you live far away
Need a shop
Whizz on in until you drop
There's gorgeous Greggs
Cheap Home Bargains
Plus many more shops.

If you live far away
Don't have a library
Check out a book
There's books for all ages
Unfortunately they don't cook.

Elizabeth Cliff (10)
Manston St James CE Primary School

Food For The Micabochis

They are coming . . .
To the humungous Micabochis,
The Crossgates Centre
Is just a big sausage
Hiding in the midst of Earth's tochi.

They are coming . . .
They eye it all the time,
A tasty new snack,
Straight from the sack,
To be eaten with wine.

They are coming . . .
The contents of this mighty feast
Are Greggs, Wilkos
And tasty Tescos,
Irresistible for the hungry beasts.

They are coming . . .
But Gamestation cries,
'No! No! No!'
Don't have a go!
And Claire's almost dies!

They are coming . . .
Their slimy bodies start to crave,
A delicious delight,
Something to bite,
The Centre's danger is grave.

They are coming . . .
Keep your distance from the Centre!
Don't stay there too long,
That would be quite wrong!
For elaborate danger may enter . . .

Ben Tailby (10)
Manston St James CE Primary School

Come To Crossgates

Come to Crossgates now,
They have a centre full of treats
But you mustn't forget sweets.
You should come to Crossgates now! But don't worry how
So why not . . .
Come to Crossgates now.

Come to Crossgates now,
You could travel here on a train,
It will be like blood running down your vein.
When you get here you will say, 'Oh wow!'
So why not . . .
Come to Crossgates now.

Come to Crossgates now,
You will love it there
Plus it's not in the middle of nowhere.
So that means there will not be a cow,
So why not . . .
Come to Crossgates now.

Come to Crossgates now,
Are you full of energy?
That is what you can do with me.
When you're done, travel home, you know how,
So why not . . .
Come to Crossgates now.

Come to Crossgates now
But before you go
Just remember go with the flow.
Now you go we take a bow,
So why not . . .
Come to Crossgates now.

Abigayle Iveson (10)
Manston St James CE Primary School

Crossgates

Come here if you live far,
Buy a ticket,
Or come in the car,
Need to shop well, look what we've got,
There's even a bar!

Come here if you live far,
Need a train,
There will be no pain,
Everyone's welcoming and will have a chat,
Just come and get a train!

Come here if you live far,
Need something to eat,
We'll go to Greggs,
Tasty delights just for you,
That's why Greggs is here for you!

Come here if you live far,
Want a book,
Well come to our library,
Get lots of books.

Come here if you live far,
Need some fun well go to Manston Park,
Slides, swings and many more,
Lots of fields to relax,
Just don't leave your apple core!

Crossgates,
Crossgates,
It's so good,
Just come, come,
It's so fun.

Emily Natasha Rice (10)
Manston St James CE Primary School

The Best Shopping Centre I Know!

I really advise you to come
To this super, fantastic place.
It's called the Crossgates Centre,
With lots of room and space.

Just wait till you walk inside . . .
And *wham!*
A hundred dazzling lights,
A silver shiny ceiling
And all the new pop singles
That give you that tingling feeling!

I really advise you to come
To this super, fantastic place.
It's the best shopping centre I know
And it gives you a happy face!

There are lots of shops in the centre
Like Peacocks, Whippys and Greggs.
The hardware shop's called Wilkos,
You can get balloons, toys and pegs.

If your cupboards are empty,
If you don't have a nice pot of tea,
Then you should go to Fultons, Tescos or Wilsons,
They make me as happy as can be

You might have run out of clothes
Or you might be going out tonight.
Then go to Buzz, New Look or Select,
They'll give you so much delight!

Hollie Burwell (10)
Manston St James CE Primary School

The Crossgates Centre

Come and enter,
The Crossgates Centre . . .
Oh my!
Look what you can buy:

I've just bought -
Some great gingerbread!
From gorgeous Greggs.

Come and enter,
The Crossgates Centre . . .
Oh my!
Look what you can buy:

I've just bought,
Magical movies!
From brilliant Blockbusters!

Come and enter,
The Crossgates Centre . . .
Oh my!
Look what you can buy:

I've just bought -
Games with greatness!
From glorious Gamestation!

Come and enter,
The Crossgates Centre . . .
Oh my!
Look what you can buy!

Matthew Jones (11)
Manston St James CE Primary School

In Crossgates

In Crossgates,
The people are weird,
Or very chilled out;
As long as they are there
Nobody will doubt.

Coe's is the fish shop,
Where people can eat
Fish and chips if they want
Or just to rest their feet.

Paws For Thought
Is an incredible place to be;
I couldn't live without it,
It's very important to me.

The park is the place
Where people can play;
Footy, racing,
Or just swinging all day.

The library is one place
Where people come to read;
Or have a little quiet time
Or do a good deed.

The school is in Manston,
That's where the park is too,
The teachers are all there
To educate you.

Sarah Driscoll (10)
Manston St James CE Primary School

The Park

The park in spring
Is bursting with colour
Of daisies and daffodils.
Animals are waking up
And scurrying over the hills.

The park in summer
Is baking hot
Yet small children still play.
Swing on the swings or slide on the slide
During the month of May!

The park in autumn
Looks bare and dead
But really it's full of life.
Just peer under a leaf or two
And you'll find some little white mice.

The park in winter
Gleaming white with snow
That lies peacefully on the grass.
Building snowmen all day long
You definitely won't want to pass.

Not a day goes by
Without someone in the park
Full of laughter and cheer.
You'll fit in perfectly without a doubt
Never ever feeling queer.

Grace Parker (10)
Manston St James CE Primary School

I Sit And Watch In Crossgates

I sit and watch
The trains go by,
On their journeys far and wide,
The way the horn hoots loud and clear,
To tell everyone they're nearly here.

I sit and watch
The children play,
Running around the park,
While mums chatter through the day,
But they're all gone by dark.

I sit and watch
The clever students
Wander in the library,
Picking out the best algebra books,
Ever so slyly.

I sit and watch
The gas tower,
Slowly moving slowly down,
Thinking of all the energy we use
In this little town.

I sit and watch
The friendly people
Moving round Crossgates,
Eating fish and chips all day,
That's why I love this place.

Harriet Pyrah (10)
Manston St James CE Primary School

Fantastic Food

Fantastic food,
Fantastic food,
That really gets you in the mood,
To eat and eat away,
It will really make your day!

Gorgeous Greggs,
Gorgeous Greggs,
Bacon, steak and eggs
And éclairs and muffins too,
You'll enjoy them the whole way through.

Cool Coe's,
Cool Coe's,
The taste never goes,
Fish butties, salty chips,
Mind out, they will widen your hips!

Wacky Wilsons,
Wacky Wilsons,
Just so delicious,
Yummy, yummy, yummy,
A treat for your tummy!

Fantastic food,
Fantastic food,
That really gets you in the mood,
To eat and eat away,
It will really make your day!

Holly Ellis (10)
Manston St James CE Primary School

Crossgates

If you're sat at home, bored and need to shop,
Come along to the Crossgates Centre
And shop until you drop!

There's so many shops to choose,
Lots of gains but never lose.
If you need a food shop come and get it here
But if you want a quiet chat, friends can whisper in your ear.

Children play in the park,
Mostly until it gets dark,
Then they get fish and chips from Coe's.

The trees blow in the wind,
Prancing and dancing around.
As the trees rustle in the wind
You never hear a sound.

In the summer children want to visit different parks,
So they hop on the train
Glad you didn't have to walk,
Will save you a lot of pain.

Go to Lacantina, for your special treat
After you have been there you'll say it was sweet.
So come to Crossgates today, shops and things to play,
Tell everyone to come here,
Then you could go for a beer.

Georgia-Mae Gaughan (10)
Manston St James CE Primary School

At The Park

At the park you can
Play on the swings or
Walk the dog.
Go on the slide or
Watch a frog.

If you're walking the dog
Be sure to go right round.
Or if you're on the frame don't fall
And hit the ground.

Play in the tennis court
Or play cricket,
And footy too
As long as it's fun
I don't care what you do!

You can climb the trees
Or hide in the bushes
And sometimes see the common
Hedgehog that hardly ever rushes.

At the park you can
Play on the swings or
Walk the dog.
Go on the slide or
Watch a frog.

Bethany Coyle (10)
Manston St James CE Primary School

Monster Poem

There is a monster in your shed,
Hobbling and gobbling until it's dead.
All the tools and wood has gone!
There was a monster in your shed,
Wibble wobble the shed has gone!

Sophie Payne (10)
Manston St James CE Primary School

Crossgates

Crossgates Centre, Crossgates Centre
Is the best place ever;
Come and see what it has for you
But come quick 'cause it's now or never.

Crossgates Centre, Crossgates Centre,
Bang, clatter, boom
Goes the security guard when he opens the doors,
Unfortunately that's one of his chores.

Crossgates station, Crossgates station,
Boys and girls going on vacation;
Thirty minutes later you'll be in York,
It's a lot faster than taking a walk.

Manston Park, Manston Park,
We don't play here in the dark.
Swings, slides, monkey bars;
I bet they don't have these on Mars.

Crossgates, Crossgates,
I live here;
It's a wonderful place
Pop in when you're near.

Daniel Jagger (11)
Manston St James CE Primary School

Happiness

I went out this morning
And I started to hear birds singing a song.
Squirrels and ants dancing in the sun.
Trees were burning from the sun,
Bushes were bouncing in the jolly good fun
While the clouds were relaxing and burning brown in the sun.
By the time I got back from staring around the world,
It was my dinner, waiting, waiting, waiting.

Olivia Scott (10)
Manston St James CE Primary School

Our Town Crossgates

Our town Crossgates
Is a great place to play with your mates,
With a park and a pet shop
And a little bookies bet shop
It's great for all the family.

Our town Crossgates
Has a big shopping centre,
For all your household needs.
There's a Gamestation and a train station,
To get from here to there.

Our town Crossgates
Has a dentist and a car wash,
With a few restaurants and doctors
To keep you in shipshape
Or to enclose you in a box,
If you act like an ape!

Our town Crossgates
Is an incredible place to be,
With lots and lots of shops
For you to explore and see.

James Jagger (10)
Manston St James CE Primary School

An Angry Place

A place where bulls break things,
A place of destruction,
Where horrible trees try to catch the stars
And make them disappear,
Where glass is smashed and the noise is
Like people breaking lots of china for no reason at all,
It destroys happiness and all other nice feelings
And that's an angry place.

Conor Ian Lawrence Lloyd (10)
Manston St James CE Primary School

Crossgates

Crossgates, Crossgates,
A wonderful place to be,
The angels look down and see,
Come here, there is so much to do,
When you get there you will say *woo.*

Crossgates, Crossgates,
Bookies, Greggs and Wilson's pies,
Go to Wilkinsons to get some supplies.
Mecca Bingo you can win a fortune there,
As well as the pet shop where you can buy a hare.

Crossgates, Crossgates,
Enter Manston Park to have a good time,
It will be like shivers are running down your spine.
Try and win Wimbledon on the tennis courts,
Or just go to Gamestation to get a toy ork.

Crossgates, Crossgates,
Make sure you come at Christmas time,
Especially at the pub where you can get some wine.
At Easter come to Thorntons,
There's so much chocolate for your sons.

William Silkstone (10)
Manston St James CE Primary School

There Is A Monster In Your House

There is a monster in your house,
It wants to munch you up,
It chomps and gobbles
Until it's gone,
He eats and eats,
Never going to sleep,
Chomp!
He's eaten you up!

Jessica Helyer (10)
Manston St James CE Primary School

Crossgates

The Crossgates Centre is great,
You might find yourself a mate.
There are lots of shops with sweets to buy,
If you are that kind of guy.

At the park you can do lots of sport,
Football, cricket, any sort.
You can play lots of tennis
But don't be the local menace.

You can go to school
Or go to the station pub and play some pool.
Why not catch the train for a ride
To see another town or seaside.

Buy a pie from Wilsons or Greggs
But watch out, you might get very fat legs.
Or fish and chips from Coe's
Or get a pepperoni pizza from Dominos.

So hang around
And there you've found
The greatest place in town!

Will Holmes (10)
Manston St James CE Primary School

There Was An Old Man Of Crossgates

There was an old man of Crossgates,
Who went to the shop with his mates.
He came home later
And fell in a crater.
That silly old man of Crossgates.

Ashley Cairns (10)
Manston St James CE Primary School

Crossgates Centre

The Crossgates Centre is the best place in town.
It welcomes all people from anywhere around;
From hardware to shoe shops, Poundworld and more,
Cafés with sandwiches that you will adore.

Enjoy your journey on the runway train,
Listen to the sounds, they never stay the same!
Chuck-a-chuck-chew, like the pitter of the rain,
Then stop at the chippy and you'll be entertained!

Bag a bargain in Tesco Metro;
You'll feel the urge to buy a little extra,
You will want to fill your trolley to the top
And never ever want to stop!

Crossgates, Crossgates, is so good,
Tell your friends to go, they should.

Now you have to say goodbye,
Do not worry and do not cry;
You'll come back once again
On Crossgates runway train!

Chloe Cooper (11)
Manston St James CE Primary School

Jaguar

Big cat, small cat, I live far,
In South America I'm a jaguar.
My coat is golden yellow with lots
Of black and brown spots.
As I stalk my prey at night,
I jump out and give them a fright.
I knock them down with my big, big paws
And rip them to shreds with my razor-sharp claws.
I shuffle my prey up the tree
And enjoy my lovely tea.

Lewis Ellwood (10)
Manston St James CE Primary School

Crossgates

Why not enter
The Crossgates Centre,
For fabulous foods galore?
Gorgeous Greggs,
Lovely Livorno's,
There's also lots, lots more!

Why not enter
The Crossgates Centre,
For awesome games and fun?
Brilliant Blockbuster,
Great Gamestation,
There's some really good games with a gun!

Now you've entered
The Crossgates Centre,
Did you like the food?
After you've played
With the cool games,
You should be in a great mood!

Owen Savage (10)
Manston St James CE Primary School

Friends

Friends are good, friends are bad,
Some of them are very sad,
Some of them are a little pest,
They sometimes fail their spelling test.

They laugh and play all of the day,
But some of them don't want to stay,
Some of them like running, some of them do not,
But some of them like the sun being very, very hot.

We are all different, we are not the same,
But we can play together, lots of funny games.

Ainslie Bell (11)
Manston St James CE Primary School

Crossgates

Crossgates is a great place to be,
Plus it's open to anybody.
Crossgates is cool, you should come;
Because at Christmas, it's double the fun.

So here are some places that are here in Crossgates:
Estate agents and library and car wash are ace.

Crossgates is a great place to be
Plus it's open to anybody.
There's also a place called the Crossgates Centre,
You'll think it's awesome as soon as you enter.

Crossgates is a great place to be
Plus it's open to anybody.
There's some good stuff for pets at Paws For Thought,
Here's some things you could have bought -
Dog food, cat food, maybe even rat food!

Crossgates is a great place to be
And I'm glad to live here!

Joel Gray (10)
Manston St James CE Primary School

My Monkey Lay On Its Tum

My monkey lay on its tum
And then danced on its bum.
Some people laughed,
Some people chuckled,
But I like her the way she is.

My monkey is silly,
My monkey is mischievous.
I like my monkey,
My funny little monkey,
Just the way she is.

Hannah Rose Broadbent (10)
Manston St James CE Primary School

All About Crossgates

Come here far or near
Crossgates is the place to be!
When the sun is shining or it's pouring down with rain
You'll still have fun when you're shopping at Crossgates.

How you get here, it doesn't matter
But there's quite a lot of transport around here
So get a bus or even a train and hop in, two minutes you'll be near.

Now let's talk about the park
And at this time of year there's lots of rotten bark.

If you come from far abroad
And you need a place to live
Just find Reed Rains
And they would find you a place.

Now that's it
I'm trying to say goodbye
So hope you come
Maybe see you soon.

Samantha Lewis (11)
Manston St James CE Primary School

Crossgates' Public Transport

Ten, ten, ten, every ten minutes,
That's how frequent the buses are,
Coming form Whinmoor or even Castleford,
Crossgates is a great place to be.

Jump off at the bus stop,
Next to the centre,
Go in, go out,
There'll be a bus waiting for you.

Waiting for a train at the station,
Then the announcer says it's late,
Oh, here it comes screeching to a stop,
Crossgates is a great place to be.

Coming on a slow one from Blackpool North,
Or on a fast one from York,
If you're coming from Inverness,
Crossgates is a great place to be.

David Gubbins (10)
Manston St James CE Primary School

Crossgates

Crossgates in general is a delightful place to be,
There's bingo, libraries and fishmongers.
But none of them are successful,
Compared to the Crossgates Centre.

The playground at the park is a brilliant place to be,
There's lots of birds and squirrels for everyone to see.
There's swings, a roundabout and a wiggly slide too,
So come and have some fun, it's there for you too.

If you ever want a pizza then Dominos is never far away,
They will give you a good supply
And you'll be quick to fly.
So if you're ever short of food,
Then pop down to Dominos.

So now I think I've proved my point,
That Crossgates is a wondrous joy.

Emily Saysell (10)
Manston St James CE Primary School

Pencil Case, Personification Poem

This morning as I was sat in my seat
My equipment and things around me started behaving badly!

My sharpener was rolling round the table
And started to shrink pencils by sharpening them!
As the pencils were crying for help at the end of the table,
The rubbers were struggling to get out of my pencil case
That had run away like a man being chased by a pack of killer dogs!
My highlighters were climbing up the window trying to get to
The nearest stationery store,
While my compasses were fighting like some angry fencers.

Later, things calmed down,
But just as I caught them all . . .

Sadie May O'Donoghue (10)
Manston St James CE Primary School

Jaguar

Sooooo lazy up in the tree all day,
Nocturnal he may be.
He may have eyes that are big and yellow
Watching your every move.
'It's time to have some breakfast, I see,'
He says when he goes down the tree.
His beautiful spotted coat is lovely as I see,
It astounds me!
He gets down *sooo* low and walks to his victim.
His big black nose can smell its death,
As he crushes its skull until it's still.
His colourful orange and yellow mixed coat,
Full of blood,
For the next day the deer awaits!

Lilly-Mae Metcalfe (10)
Manston St James CE Primary School

Horrid Henry!

He is very mad,
But never sad!
He has a perfect brother,
And wants him to suffer.
He is always naughty,
Mum and Dad are the big forty!
Peter I want to kill
So does my best friend Will.
He has a gigantic mouth
What travels down south?
He has a big cat
What sits on the cream mat?
He has a good den
But wants a hen!

Josie Tomkinson (10)
Micklefield CE Primary School

The Dragon

He swoops up high,
High in the sky,
To terrorise below
And when he destroys all villages,
He is never slow.

He lives in a cave,
While destruction he craves.
He stays day after day,
From April to May,
(And longer).

He snacks on sheep,
Who jump and leap,
To get out of his paths.
The amount he eats,
As you may see,
Is some pretty hard maths.

His fiery breath
Can cause certain death,
While his bright green scales
Like the forest of Wales,
Flash with brilliant colour.
Which is all too good,
'Cause it blinds the sheep,
Which only makes him fuller.

Jacob Burley (10)
Micklefield CE Primary School

Love

Love is red like a rose freshly picked.
Love tastes fluffy like candyfloss.
Love smells like a chocolate cake sizzling in the oven.
Love looks beautiful, like a face in the mirror.

Kirsty Webster (10)
Micklefield CE Primary School

Happiness

Happiness is yellow like a rose sitting in a huge field.
Happiness tastes like sugary chocolate cupcakes
sitting on a happy plate.
Happiness smells like delicious sweet strawberries.
Happiness looks like children having lots of fun in the sea
on a sunny day.
Happiness sounds loud like birds cheeping.
Happiness feels soft like fluffy birds' feathers.

Abbigail Walsh (9)
Micklefield CE Primary School

The Teddy

I get cuddled every night,
I get squeezed nice and tight.
You keep me warm in the duvet
And lots of games we play.
I have lots of cuddly friends,
Our friendship never ends.
I'm very fluffy and I'm soft
But when a new one comes along I'm stuffed in the loft.

Natalie Keeble (10)
Micklefield CE Primary School

Love

Love is red, like beautiful roses.
It tastes like juicy red strawberries mixed with chocolate cake.
It looks like a lovely sunny street with nice cold swimming pools in.
It feels great, like you have just won the lottery.
It sounds peaceful, like babies sleeping.
It smells gorgeous, like Sunday dinner.

Callum Turner (10)
Micklefield CE Primary School

Love

Love is red like a beautiful rose
Love tastes lovely like pink candyfloss
Love smells gorgeous like Christmas pudding
Love looks like a big love heart in the sky
Love sounds like calming wedding music
Love feels warm like the sun on a summer's day.

Shannon Douglass (9)
Micklefield CE Primary School

Happiness

Happiness is yellow like the hot sunshine
Happiness tastes nice like creamy chocolate
Happiness smells beautiful like a red rose
Happiness sounds quiet like falling leaves
Happiness feels soft like a cuddly bear.

Jordan Horner Pugh (9)
Micklefield CE Primary School

Hate

Hate is black like a stormy cloud.
It tastes like salty seawater.
Hate smells like sour milk.
It looks like an ugly goblin.
Hate sounds like thunder crashing.

Samuel Short (9)
Micklefield CE Primary School

Kangaroo-Me

I am in the new world
New surroundings, everything twirled and curled
I wondered where I was
Then I was greeted by a friendly wasp
The wasp showed me everything I needed to see
The wasp took me to a really big pine tree
We ventured up it as high as could be
I looked at the view and thought what a beautiful scene
We climbed back down
Looking all around
For what else we could do
Then we spotted a very blue kangaroo
We walked over not knowing what to do
So we improvised and cheered him up
We went out and bought him a pup
Then suddenly
Everything went blurry
I woke up with something very furry
It was a dog called Curly
I remembered it was my birthday
Only just yesterday
I was feeling really blue
But my parents didn't really know what to do
So they decided to cheer me up
By getting me a little pup.

Jert Serrano (10)
St Augustine's RC Primary School, Leeds

A Poem About Bullies

The colossal figures
Like gigantic diggers,
The pain drove me insane,
I cried out in vain,
The cuts on my face,
The blood on my laces,
All because of my race,
Every day the pushing and shoving,
The suffering in silence,
Feeling the violence,
Jumping over the fence were the bullies in hoodies stealing 55 pence,
The park was my favourite place to cry,
Trying hard to dry my eyes,
Upon my face left a scar,
Every time I think about it my heart seems to race.

Tseyyin Chan (11)
St Augustine's RC Primary School, Leeds

Mary's Wish!

Mary's mum is a great cook
And she loves a good book,
But Mary's dad is cruel and mean,
So he slaps her on her cheeks,
If she gets one step in his way, he would say,
'Go to bed and don't come out until May.'
She loves her mum but she hates her dad,
Because he is always saying she's been bad,
She hates her life and she is talking to you,
She even still has her saggy old shoe,
She wishes she could go and leave him in her past,
So this time has to go fast, fast, fast.

Courtney Longstaff (11)
St Augustine's RC Primary School, Leeds

Lost

I am walking down a steamy pathway,
Is it 6 o'clock? Is it Monday?
I have not had a drink or been fed,
No one knows if I am alive or dead.
My mum and dad are worried at home,
As I walk on the mountain's dome.
It is really misty and cold,
No one to see, no one to hold.
The kiss of my mum, the hug of my dad,
I wish someone could see, how I feel so sad.
The silent touch of frost,
Now I know, how it feels to be lost.
My hot, salty tears stroll down my cheek,
Can't I just give my house a little peek.
The mountain is so empty, I can't build a den,
I wish I was safe back home again.

Zoya Nadeem (11)
St Augustine's RC Primary School, Leeds

Tiger

Striped body
Bone cruncher
Meat eater
Fast runner
Brilliant predator
Long leaper
High jumper
Super spotter
Fantastic hider
Strong muscles
Sharp claws
Loud *roarer!*

Alan Joseph (10)
St Augustine's RC Primary School, Leeds

Some Flowers Are . . .

Some flowers are red
As they stay in a bed

Some flowers are pink
They make the boys wink

Some flowers are blue
They remind me of you

Some flowers are green
They remind me of the Queen

Some flowers are grey
They make you sad all day

Some flowers are gold
They are big, bright and bold.

Megan Haynes (10)
St Augustine's RC Primary School, Leeds

Homework

Homework is helpful,
But for me it's dreadful.

I've got diving lessons at five,
I've got to go there and dive.

I've got to bring it in tomorrow,
But the only way is to borrow.

The worst homework is literacy,
The best homework is numeracy.

In literacy I've got to write a story,
In numeracy I've got to do symmetry.

Now I've finished and done my best,
I can have a long big rest.

Alby Joseph (10)
St Augustine's RC Primary School, Leeds

The Red Cloak

Passed on from generation to generation,
Handcrafted and imported to a small nation.

Found in America just to be sold
To a rich lady who was very old.

Before she died she gave it away
To her granddaughter who was named May.

Years went by 'til 1974,
The red cloak found on a sunny beach shore.

A boy found it and gave it for free
To a quite small family of three.

The red cloak was floating on the sea
And since that day it belonged to me.

Abby Gaile Masangya (11)
St Augustine's RC Primary School, Leeds

The Rose

As I gaze I ponder upon this perfect thing,
What purpose does a rose have?
Except to bless and bring
Upliftment to the spirit
When jaded, tired and sore,
To gladden and refresh us
With its presence - nothing more.

Did God make flowers for healing?
I'm sure it's in His plan,
To speak through His created things
And touch the heart of Man.

Brandon Kavanagh
St Augustine's RC Primary School, Leeds

Swaps

I will give you
A new friend,
A spider,
A piece of bubblegum without an end,
A glider,
A bend, (I don't know how I'll give you that!
I'll give you it as soon as I find out what it is)
For your brand new shoes,
So have we got a deal?

No!

Alycia Browne (10)
St Augustine's RC Primary School, Leeds

Nothing To Do

Just got home, done my homework.
Had my tea and there is nothing to see.
Sat by the fire watching TV,
Mum's shouting at me for not listening to her sing.
Playing ping-pong with my dad.
Brother's upstairs having a bath.
Sister's at a party, out and about.
Nana's here, stressing a lot, never sitting down.
Cleaning up, not much harm.

Olivia O'Toole (10)
St Augustine's RC Primary School, Leeds

I Wonder Why . . .?

I wonder why the moon is white,
I wonder why the sun is bright,
I wonder why the sky is blue,
I wonder why Heaven is true,
I wonder why birds fly in the sky,
I wonder when this poem will end,
Maybe at the weekend.

Anne Roxas (11)
St Augustine's RC Primary School, Leeds

Anger

It sounds like booming thunder that never ends,
It feels like you want to push all over again and again,
It smells like dark grey smoke is running up your nose like mad men,
It looks like a ring of fire is surrounding you and you can never get out,
It makes me feel scrunched up like a piece of paper,
It's like doing something you hate, like tidying up,
It tastes like a hot chilli pepper, hotter than ever,
It sounds like millions of babies crying together
And you can't move!

Adam Saville (9)
Stanningley Primary School

Fear

It smells like a ghostly acid!
It looks like a two-headed demon!
It tastes like bitter medicine!
It feels like an edged cliff!
It sounds like a howling wolf!
It is like a dentist giving you a filling!
It reminds me of getting attacked by two Alsatians!

Thomas Sheldon (9)
Stanningley Primary School

Love

It feels like a hot bubbly bath,
It smells like a glass of red wine,
It is like a sun smiling at me,
It sounds like a bird singing in my ear,
It looks like a red rose,
It reminds me of when I was born,
It tastes like a romantic dinner,
It tastes like a big chocolate cake,
It makes me glad I was born.

Chloe Warren (9)
Stanningley Primary School

The Emotion

Love
It feels like a sweet kiss in the summer,
It looks like a red rose popping out at you,
It smells like a bunch of flowers,
It is like a summer holiday,
It reminds me of my mum's hugs,
It smells like wonderful perfume,
It sounds like a slow song,
It always makes me smile.

Sophie Poulter (9)
Stanningley Primary School

Happiness

It sounds like children singing sweetly.
It smells like the sweet smell of chocolate cake.
It looks like a crystal blue waterfall on a hot summer's day.
It feels like the golden bright sand on the beach.
It tastes like a hot chilli pepper, sweeter than ever.
It looks like a tall mountain.

Joe Pearce (9)
Stanningley Primary School

What Is Worry . . .

It is like your world is crumbling to pieces,
It sounds like a thunderous roar in my ears,
It feels like a racing heart pounding against my chest,
It smells like smoke from a roaring fire,
It looks like smoke filling the air around me,
It reminds me of a tremendous storm,
It makes me feel like I forget everything . . .

That is worry.

Chloe Moore (10)
Stanningley Primary School

The Loved Poem

It sounds like bluebirds tweeting a song.
It tastes like cake covered in cream.
It feels like having a big hug from my mummy.
It smells like red roses on a hot summer day.
It reminds me of when I saw Hanna.
It looks like my baby sister Hanna.
It is like I am having 200 hugs.
It always makes me think of Hanna.

Jessica Dixon (9)
Stanningley Primary School

The Happiness Poem!

It sounds like someone kissing me on the lips.
It feels like a soft cuddly bear coming towards me.
It smells like some lovely perfume.
It reminds me of a nice shiny beach.
It looks like a big cuddly blanket.
It is like my mum is giving me a hug.
It always makes me happy.

Zara Towey (9)
Stanningley Primary School

Love

It sounds like sweet birds singing in the garden on a hot
summer's day.
It feels like I'm hypnotised.
It smells like the golden perfume everyone wants.
It reminds me of the best thing in the world.
It looks like the cutest pup ever.
It is like one million birds in the air.
It always makes me feel special.

Callum Corless (9)
Stanningley Primary School

The Lover

It feels like hot melted chocolate,
It smells like a sweet summer glass of wine,
It reminds me of my little puppy,
It feels like a wonderful sweet kiss,
It's like a dream with rainbows and everything,
It smells like a big red rose,
It's like birds singing together.

Joe Makin (9)
Stanningley Primary School

The Scary Fear Poem

It is like I'm getting hit by fire.
It sounds like a dragon getting ready to bite.
It feels like I'm frozen.
It reminds me of someone who bullied me.
It looks like something going to attack.
It always makes me cry.
It feels like I'm going to melt from fire.

Sam Law (10)
Stanningley Primary School

Believing

It is like a believing hand,
It looks like the world caring for us,
It smells like beautiful flowers in summer,
It feels like a soft, fluffy cat,
It sounds like small pretty birds singing to me,
It always makes me feel protected,
It reminds me of knowing I have friends.

Brandon Almond (10)
Stanningley Primary School

This Is The Poem Of Fear

It is like someone stabbing you,
It sounds like a howling wolf at midnight,
It feels like you are burning,
It smells like a rotten egg,
It looks like massive fiery flames,
It reminds me of the worst day of my life,
It always makes me jump into my bed.

Kane Davey (9)
Stanningley Primary School

Love

It is like children singing,
It smells like red roses,
It looks like a wedding day,
It tastes like sweets,
It feels like hands,
It reminds me of when I had my first kiss,
It always makes me happy.

Kia McClarty (9)
Stanningley Primary School

Fear

It sounds like a thunderous wolf coming to me,
It feels like a pile of old rough paper,
It smells like the sun falling into Earth,
It looks like a giant crowd of children singing badly,
It reminds me of a giant ball of thunder,
It always makes me upset when I see it,
It tastes like hot and spicy chicken.

Leah Lazar (9)
Stanningley Primary School

Anger Poem!

It looks like a mad grey lightning cloud.
It tastes like the bitterness of rotten milk.
It smells like a horrible black bin up close.
It feels like a bumpy sharp wall.
It reminds me of punching someone.
It makes me want to go to bed forever.

Callum Rawson (9)
Stanningley Primary School

Happiness

It sounds like a bird singing in a tree.
It feels like a cuddly bear.
It smells like brand new.
It looks like a tropical drink.
It is like a cuddly blanket.
It reminds me of my two cats.

Ellis Whiteley (9)
Stanningley Primary School

Love Poem

It sounds like tweeting birds in the sun.
It feels like a boiling feeling in my tummy.
It smells like fresh roses from a rose bush.
It reminds me of my mum giving me a big hug.
It tastes like delicious chocolates.
It always makes me faint.

Millie Adams (10)
Stanningley Primary School

Happiness

It sounds like the sound of chirping birds in a brand new morning.
It feels like the fluffiness of a brand new kitten on a weekend.
It smells like the sweet scent of aftershave on a very sunny day.
It reminds me of when I first got my cute dog.
It always makes me have a warm tummy.

Niall Rowlands (9)
Stanningley Primary School

Comparing England And Africa

In England we have shops that we can go to
And we can buy anything we want.
In Africa they will probably have to walk miles to go to a market.
In England we have shoes that we can play out in
And go to important places in.
In Africa they don't have shoes to play out in
And go to important places in.
In England we have food, money and jobs.
In Africa they don't have money or good food or jobs.
In England we are not poor but some people are.
In Africa most people are poor but some people have some money.
In England we have clean water from the tap.
In Africa they will have to walk miles to get some water.

Amiee-Leigh Crossley (9)
Swinnow Primary School

We Have A Wonderful World

I want to live in a world where differences are accepted
Why do people have to bully
Just because other people are different
Because their skin is a different colour
Or they have problems or they are disabled?

I want to live in a world with no fighting
Why do people have to fight?
Why can't we live in peace?
Instead of using guns and knives
People should be friendly
And never fight or use weapons that don't need to be used.

I want to live in a clean world
Where nobody litters
And everybody keeps our world clean.
Instead of dropping litter on the floor
Put it in the bin
And keep our world clean.

I want to live in a world with no racism
So people don't get bullied
Just because their skin is a different colour
And because their clothes are ripped and torn.
Why can't people treat them
Like they treat us?

Lewis Thorpe (9)
Swinnow Primary School

Autumn

The sky is the colour of the blue in the rainbow.
The clouds are as white as paper.
The wind sounds like a howling dog.
The trees are as bendy as jelly on a plate.
The leaves are smooth, sticky toffee.

Scarlett Brayshaw
Swinnow Primary School

What A Wonderful World

I want to live in a world with world peace
Where people don't get picked on because they're named Stacey,
Jessica or Reece.

I want to live in a world with no wars
Without people who carry around knives, guns and saws.

I want to live in a world where people do not litter
Where friends go out for dinner, whether it's sweet, sour or bitter.

I want to live in a world where people are treated the same
And no being bullied or picked on, being called lame.

I want to live in a world where everyone works as a team
Where no one is nasty or mean.

I want to live in a world with no pollution
Where things were explained properly, so there's no confusion.

I want to live in a world where there's no racist abuse
And everything is put to a truce.

I want to live in a wonderful world.

Megan Dover (9)
Swinnow Primary School

Autumn

The leaves are as slippy as a banana skin.
The squirrels run up and down a tree like a mad dog.
The wind whistles like a kettle when the water has boiled.
The weather is as chilly as an ice pop.
The night sky is as black as a witch's cat.
The grass is as green as lettuce.
The sky is as blue as the ocean.
The twigs are as dry as a baby's cheek.
The wind is as cool as Snoop Dogg.

Tori Mitchell
Swinnow Primary School

People With Differences

I wear jeans and T-shirts,
You might wear a football kit,
If you have glasses it does not matter,
We are all the same.

People might not have enough money to have posh clothes,
People might have money to buy Nike and Puma,
But it doesn't matter what you wear,
We are all the same.

It doesn't matter if you have a big or a little house,
It doesn't matter if you have small or giant families,
It doesn't matter if you're black or white,
We are all the same.

It doesn't matter if you are old,
It doesn't matter if you are young,
It doesn't matter if you are wrinkled,
We are all the same.

Rebecca Smith (10)
Swinnow Primary School

A Perfect World

A perfect world would be where war never was.
A perfect world would be where people would never die.
A perfect world would be where people would never litter.

A perfect world would be where floods and tsunamis would
never happen.
A perfect world would be where fires never happened.
A perfect world would be where animals wouldn't get hunted.

A perfect world would be where guns, knives and drugs didn't exist.
A perfect world would be where everyone would be vegetarians.
A perfect world would be where money grew on trees.

This is a perfect world that I would like to live in.

Benjamin Crook (9)
Swinnow Primary School

A Lost Quiet Evacuee

I felt like a lost child always crying, I was so upset!
Listening to everything before I went.
I was so scared, crying endlessly in the station
When the train came rolling in.
The train I was going to was a ghost town, I was crying so much,
I wished I could stay.
I am an evacuee clinging to my mum in the station.

I felt sick because I was going to leave her, I couldn't believe
I was getting dragged away in a blur.
I was scarred with this for life but I was old enough to understand.
This was the worst time I had had but I had to go, I wasn't glad,
I am an evacuee clinging to my mum in the station.

I know that I needed to go, it was so upsetting and depressing.
I'm lonely, scared with my lovely mum and dad out of my life.
I sometimes think why?
And know something has been stolen from my life.

Michelle Yates (10)
Swinnow Primary School

The Lost Soul

I felt like my soul had disappeared.
As I tensed all my muscles I rapidly began to cry.
I felt I would explode with tears.
I am an evacuee, words can't describe it.

I felt like jumping out the window.
I was totally destroyed.
I felt speechless, all you could hear was crying.
I am an evacuee, words can't describe it.

I could smell all the animals on the farm.
The countryside was bright but I felt dark inside.
The place where he lives is small but lively.
I am an evacuee words can't describe it.

Ben Lawrence (10)
Swinnow Primary School

An Evacuee With An Unsettled Mind

I feel as if it's all a dream.
My heart is full of misery.
I may never kiss my parents' cheeks again.
I'm an evacuee, with an unsettled mind.

On the station things were going through my mind.
My mum could get bombed, anytime.
How could I leave her in this state.
I'm an evacuee, with an unsettled mind.

We arrived, what a fright a strange woman was standing straight and upright.
My mama was far behind in Leeds, she was gone.
I was then to follow a man with long legs and strange eyes.
I'm an evacuee, with an unsettled mind.

Rebecca Mail (10)
Swinnow Primary School

The Half Broken Life

I am at the train station saying goodbye to my mum
I won't forget this day as long as I live
I am as lonely as anyone would be
I am an evacuee, when will I see my mum again?

I have been torn away from my mum
It's not fair
It's like a heart, snapped in half
I am thinking about when my mum will write to me
I am an evacuee, when will I see my mum again?

Getting off the train with dismay I see
My owner standing there, waiting for me
He says, 'Come on.'
I am an evacuee, when will I see my mum again?

Melissa Booth (10)
Swinnow Primary School

The Boy In Rags

I had to leave my mum behind.
I could taste the smoke of the train.
I could hear all the children shouting and screaming.
I am a small evacuee.

It was very heartbreaking watching my mum's figure get smaller
and smaller.

I was crying, my eyes were red raw.
It was very heartbreaking watching my mum's figure get smaller
and smaller.

I am a small evacuee.

I could see the countryside bright and as beautiful as can be.
I could taste the fresh air as bright as can be.
I could smell the nice white bread so fresh from the bakeries.
I am a small evacuee.

Ethan White (10)
Swinnow Primary School

The Intimidated Boy

It was the worst day of my life.
I was sick with fear, I began to cry, but I really didn't want to die.
It was time to go on the train, I was so upset it was insane.
I am an evacuee, it is madness.

When I got on the train it was crowded.
Kids crying, parents waving, I was lost.
I rushed to a window to wave goodbye,
But she'd already started to cry.
I am an evacuee, it is madness.

When I got there at 3.15, I really needed a wee.
When I got off the train I was met by Elaine.
She was very nice, very kind but she can be bossy at times.
I am an evacuee, it is madness.

Adam Smith (11)
Swinnow Primary School

Our Perfect World

I want to live in a world with peace and harmony.
Each country settles its differences.
War is a thing of the past.
This is our world of happiness.

I want to live in a world where everyone
And everything is protected.
In my world, money should not matter.
Jobs are available to everyone.
This is our world of happiness.

I want to live in a world where global warming has been prevented.
Diseases such as cancer are wiped out.
Food and water is always there.
This is our world of happiness.

Jonathan Smith (9)
Swinnow Primary School

Away From Home!

I felt in despair when my mum left me alone.
I tasted salty tears in the back of my throat.
I felt curious why my mum couldn't come too.
I am an evacuee, confused and homesick.

The train left the sight of my mum, I was petrified and worried.
My brother was holding me tight because he had just suffered a fright.
All I could hear was the sound of the train going fast in the rain.
I am an evacuee, confused and homesick.

I met an old man who had a dog called Sam.
A gas mask hanging at my side, I thought of my mum and cried.
He had a friendly cottage and a very big vegetable patch.
I am an evacuee, confused and homesick.

Jessica Healy-Jacques (11)
Swinnow Primary School

I Want To Live In A World

I want to live in a world with peace and harmony,
Each country settles its differences,
War is a thing of the past,
This is our world of happiness.

I want to live in a world where everyone respects everyone
And everything,
In my world money should not matter,
Jobs are available to everyone,
This is our world of happiness.

I want to live in a world where global warming has been prevented,
Diseases such as cancer are wiped out,
Food and water are always there,
This is our perfect world of happiness.

Shelley Cook (9)
Swinnow Primary School

A Very Lonely Evacuee

My mum was crying and very upset, that made me sad.
Tears ran down my face as my mother's sadness showed.
I was crying as my mam kissed me goodbye.
I am an evacuee, lonely and scared.

As I got dragged away from my mother,
Tears were streaming down my face.
As I said goodbye I straight away started to cry.
I cried, knowing that I may never see my mam again.
I am an evacuee, lonely and scared.

I got off the train but was still thinking about my mother.
I was still upset as I was smelling the smoke.
As my guardian told me to follow them I suddenly turned shy.
I am an evacuee, lonely and scared.

Elisha Oxley-Waterson (11)
Swinnow Primary School

The Destroyed Evacuee

I was speechless, my mum's life could end here.
I was in despair, I broke down into tears.
I was nervous, I would never see my mum again.
I am an evacuee, I want the war to stop.

The train came round the corner, I clung onto my mum.
I got on the train, I was lonely, I did not know anyone.
The train pulled away, my mum went out of sight.
I am an evacuee, I want the war to stop.

Arriving at the countryside was a new experience.
A man stood in front of me, 'Come on I ain't got all day.'
The house was all nice and posh, it could be worth a little dosh.
I am an evacuee, I want the war to stop.

Adam Robinson (10)
Swinnow Primary School

The Pained Evacuee

I really don't want to go away.
I'll hate being an evacuee.
The train lights glared at me.
I am an evacuee, lonely and homesick.

Why couldn't my mum go with me?
Neville Chamberlain was very wrong
I want the war to stop.
I am an evacuee, lonely and homesick.

We got off at a large station.
I didn't know where I was.
I was then given my belongings.
I am an evacuee, lonely and homesick.

Ben Clayton (10)
Swinnow Primary School

The Timid Evacuee

I felt depressed, scared, worried, I am an evacuee
I just didn't want to go, I didn't want to leave
I felt like my heart was going to explode
I am an evacuee, I have gone through so much.

I heard my mum shouting me, I just couldn't turn back
I wish I weren't bad and I wish I wasn't slack
I just watched as my mum disappeared
I am an evacuee, I have gone through so much.

When I arrived I felt lost, confused and depressed
I saw all the people and houses, I didn't know where I was
I had to follow this strange man, I couldn't keep up
I am an evacuee, I have gone through so much.

Bethany Milner (10)
Swinnow Primary School

I Want To Live In A World

I want peace in my world
Where people are kind and sharing, caring
No wars, just love and helpfulness
No fighting, no bullying, no littering, no kidnapping.

No knives, no guns, no killing especially no hate
Where people use manners
No name calling and no committing suicide
No racism and no conflict.

I want no naughty people in my world
No wars just love and peace
Where people have imagination
Where there are happy families.

Owen Carson (9)
Swinnow Primary School

The Devastating Blitz

I feel like I don't have a life.
I am in despair whilst I'm being torn away.
I feel distraught and devastated at the same time.
I am an evacuee, I want my life back.

I could see my mum was depressed when we set off.
I am on the train, I am alone and petrified.
I am nauseous but still I am cautious.
I am an evacuee, I want my life back.

My guardians are quite stunned, I am also anxious.
They can see that I am tense, so they are trying to comfort me.
They are confusing me with what they're doing.
I am an evacuee, I want my life back.

Charlie Jones (10)
Swinnow Primary School

The Lost Child

I felt petrifyingly devastated when I got left
I thought that my life was not meant to be
I felt absolutely hopeless like I just did theft
I am an evacuee; poor, confused, lonely and lost.

The train I entered overflowed with despair
As the huge train pulled away I was so nauseous
This was the time my normal life had no care
I am an evacuee; poor, confused, lonely and lost.

When I arrived I had my head under my knees
As my loneliness came over me a gent and lady came with a key
When I was taking the pain it was like stealing with a high cost
I am an evacuee; poor, confused, lonely and lost.

Thomas Chaney (10)
Swinnow Primary School

I Want To Live In A World

I want to live in a world where there is peace
Where there is sharing and caring
Where people are fair and they are loving
Where people are always kind and helpful

Where the war stops and they shake hands
Where people do not bully, fight and litter
Where people are not angry and they don't commit suicide
Where there is no name calling and no poisonous spiders

Where there is happy people and happy families
No racism or being unfair and no killing
No guns and no knives and no hate
No conflict and no punching and kicking.

Brett Smith (9)
Swinnow Primary School

The Heartbroken Evacuee

I had to leave my mum and dad behind.
All the children and me were crying.
I thought I might not see my family again.
I am a very confused evacuee.

On the station I felt tears running down my face,
I got torn from my family and put on a train.
I was thinking of my parents every second.
I am a very confused evacuee.

I arrived in a very strange place, it was like a ghost town.
All the children were crying and sobbing.
I felt homesick and wanted to go back home.
I am a very confused evacuee.

James Harmson (10)
Swinnow Primary School

The Evacuee With A Missing Piece

One cold winter's day I got taken away.
I felt miserable and worried, I began to cry.
My mum and dad I'd left behind.
I am an evacuee with a missing piece.

I got on the train and found a seat.
I opened the train window and said, 'Bye Mum, love you.'
As the train pulled away, I could hear children crying.
I am an evacuee with a missing piece.

We arrived at the station and all got out.
The people all began to shout.
Where was I?
I'm an evacuee with a missing piece.

Thomas Scott (10)
Swinnow Primary School

Comparing England And Africa

England has lots of schools.
Africans don't. What Africans have is only work.
No massive schools like England but only one big hall.
In England we have lots of toys, fancy restaurants
And lots of money.
But Africans have no money, no fancy restaurants
And one or two toys.
England has white skin but Africans have black skin.
I want everything fair.
A lot of things are important to me.
We are the same inside our body!
It doesn't matter if our colours are different.

Naomi Walsh (9)
Swinnow Primary School

A Happy World

A world where we live in happiness,

H ate is eliminated,
A world where there is no violence,
P eaceful and happy world,
P eople are kind and wonderful,
Y ou don't commit crime.

W here there is no conflict,
O ur world must be tidy,
R oads and cars are safe,
L ollipops and sweets for a treat,
D on't be horrible, don't be nasty, but be glad.

Ryan Bennett (9)
Swinnow Primary School

Living In A perfect World

Living in a perfect world would be . . .
No name calling about your name if you're named
Fred, Frank or Eric.
No committing suicide, gun crime and no war.
No violent shops.
No killing animals, no kidnapping and no killing wildlife for meat.

Please God please do these things for me.

Also no following children, no smacking your children
And no shouting at people.

Please God please do these things for me.

Adam Slater (9)
Swinnow Primary School

Autumn

The leaves are as brown as a cockroach's back.
The trees are as multicoloured as the rainbow.
The toffee apples are as sweet as honey.
The sky is as orange as a fruit.
The leaves are as dead as a lost soul.
The wind is as chilly as an ice cube.
The birds are as chirpy as my mum singing in the shower.
The grass is as wavy as the sea.

Shannon Howard (8)
Swinnow Primary School

A Peaceful World

I want to live in a world where there are lovely flowers
When a healthy baby is born every hour.

I want to live in a world with lots of food for everyone
Where there's people playing and having fun.

We would all love to live in a world, where we all get along with each other
With people coming home to their father and their mother.

Courtney Mitchell (9)
Swinnow Primary School

Autumn

The branches are like static hair in a lightning storm.
The leaves are as slippery as a snail trail in the rain.
The leaves are as orange as a pumpkin.
The sky is as grey as a grey dog.
The pine cones are as brown as coffee.
The grass is as damp as a soaking towel.
The leaves are as red as a cherry.

Jessica Oldfield (8)
Swinnow Primary School

Live In A Happy World

I want to live in a world where people can have fun.
I want to live in a world where you can't fight.
I want to live in a world where people don't cry.
I want to live in a world where people share and care.
I want to live in a world with peace.
I want to live in a world with people that help when you're stuck.

Aaliyah Allen (9)
Swinnow Primary School

Autumn

Leaves are crispy like Rice Krispies.
Leaves are as yellow as a banana.
Leaves are as crunchy as crisps.
Leaves feel soft like my jumpers.
Leaves are crackling like Coco Pops.
Leaves feel smooth like a bed sheet!

Jordan Macdonald (9)
Swinnow Primary School

Autumn

The leaves are golden as the shimmering stars in the night sky.
The grass is as green as a yummy mint ice cream.
The bark is as brown as a delicious chocolate swirl.
The nuts are as brown as a brown baby's smooth bottom.
The breeze is as windy as a twisting tornado.
The rain is as heavy as a fully loaded suitcase.

Cory Blakey (9)
Swinnow Primary School

Differences In People

People are tall and people are small,
Some people are disabled and some are not,
You might have dark hair or maybe light,
You could have brown eyes or you might have blue,
They are all different just like you.

Benjamin Twyford (9)
Swinnow Primary School

Autumn

The trees in autumn start to go multicoloured as a rainbow.
The leaves are as brown as a cockroach's back.
The leaves are as red as a Manchester United kit.
The grass is as green as a crocodile.
The weather is just like Mother Nature crying.

Dylan Cartman (8)
Swinnow Primary School

Autumn

The leaves are as crunchy as Walkers crisps.
The trees are as multicoloured as a rainbow.
The wind sounds like the spirit of Mother Nature.
The nights are as black as a witch's cauldron.
The leaves are as yellow as a banana skin.

Ashton Woodhead (8)
Swinnow Primary School

Autumn

The icy mornings are as cold as a bowl of strawberry ice cream.
The wheat is as golden as a rapper's bling bling chain.
The leaves are as brown as a bronze award.
The veins of the leaves start to show like the bones of a skeleton.

William Tiffin (9)
Swinnow Primary School

Young Writers Information

We hope you have enjoyed reading this book - and that you will continue to enjoy it in the coming years.

If you like reading and writing poetry drop us a line, or give us a call, and we'll send you a free information pack.

Alternatively if you would like to order further copies of this book or any of our other titles, then please give us a call or log onto our website at www.youngwriters.co.uk.

Young Writers Information
Remus House
Coltsfoot Drive
Peterborough
PE2 9JX
(01733) 890066